STORYTELLING

PETER LANG
New York • Washington, D.C./Baltimore • Bern
Frankfurt am Main • Berlin • Brussels • Vienna • Oxford

STORYTELLING

Interdisciplinary & Intercultural Perspectives

EDITED BY
**Irene Maria F. Blayer
& Monica Sanchez**

PETER LANG
New York • Washington, D.C./Baltimore • Bern
Frankfurt am Main • Berlin • Brussels • Vienna • Oxford

Library of Congress Cataloging-in-Publication Data

Storytelling: interdisciplinary and intercultural perspectives /
edited by Irene Maria F. Blayer and Monica Sanchez.
p. cm.
Includes bibliographical references and index.
1. Storytelling. 2. Intercultural communication.
I. Blayer, Irene Maria F. II. Sanchez, Monica.
GR72.3 .S78   808.5'43—dc21   00-031321
ISBN 0-8204-5125-8

Die Deutsche Bibliothek-CIP-Einheitsaufnahme

Storytelling: interdisciplinary and intercultural perspectives /
ed. by: Irene Maria F. Blayer and Monica Sanchez.
–New York; Washington, D.C./Baltimore; Bern;
Frankfurt am Main; Berlin; Brussels; Vienna; Oxford: Lang.
ISBN 0-8204-5125-8

Cover design by Lisa Dillon

The paper in this book meets the guidelines for permanence and durability
of the Committee on Production Guidelines for Book Longevity
of the Council of Library Resources.

© 2002 Peter Lang Publishing, Inc., New York

All rights reserved.
Reprint or reproduction, even partially, in all forms such as microfilm,
xerography, microfiche, microcard, and offset strictly prohibited.

Printed in the United States of America

Table of Contents

Illustrations..vii

Preface...ix

Acknowledgments...xi

1 Stones on the Mountain: Crossing Borders into a Story
  Kay Stone...1

2 Lost in a Story: Modeling Storytelling and Storylistening
  Brian W. Sturm..14

3 Tracking the Limits of Interpretation: A Reading of the
  Novels of Umberto Eco
  Corrado Federici..27

4 Voices of Conscience: The Power of Language in the Latin
  American *Testimonio*
  Elena De Costa..41

5 On the Trail of an Arctic Tale: Tracing Sir John Franklin
  in Charles Dickens and Wilkie Collins's *The Frozen Deep*
  Erika Behrisch...58

6 Constructing the Witch
  Karen Seago..72

7 The Medieval Legend of the *Eaten Heart*
  Ernesto Virgulti...86

8 The *Geist* of the Grimms
  Allyson Wenzowski and Debi Keir-Nicholson......................102

9 Rhyme as Reason: Conjunct Verbs in Ojibwe Storytelling
  Nila Friedberg...118

10 Voices, Morals, and Identity in the Conversational
Narratives of Ten-to-Twelve-Year-Olds
Janet Maybin..130

11 A Man Amongst Men: The Intersection of Verbal, Visual,
and Vocal Elements in an Oral Narrative
Joan Swann...145

List of Contributors..162

Index..166

Illustrations

Figures

Storylistening Experience Model 19
Storylistening Trance Model 23
Versions of the *Eaten Heart* Legend 94
Edvard Munch, *Der Kuss / The Kiss*, 1902. 103
Ernst Barlach, *Der Übergang / The Transition*, 1917. 103
Emil Nolde, *Ziehende Krieger / Marching Warriors*, 1917. 104
Otto Dix, *Leonie*, 1923. 104

Tables

Independent Verbs 125
Conjunct Verbs 125
Comparison of *The Stray Cat* and *The Bird's Nest* 137
Words uttered by different personae in *A Man Amongst Men* 148
Speaking turns taken by different characters 149
Switching between different personae in *A Man Amongst Men* 152
"Taking on" and "taking off" distinction, example 1 154
"Taking on" and "taking off" distinction, example 2 155
Interpenetration of narrator and character personae, example 1 156
Interpenetration of narrator and character personae, example 2 157
Interpenetration of narrator and character personae, example 3 157

Preface

Stories are the threads that weave cohesion into our existence. They link us to both our ancestors and our descendants. Storytelling itself is "the fundamental instrument of thought" (Mark Turner, *The Literary Mind*); it is what allows an individual to create his or her personal identity and what permits a society to develop its communal story. This field of study has benefited from a wide range of disciplines. Researchers hail from anthropology, communication and media studies, education, folklore, history, linguistics, modern languages and literature, and performance arts, among others. Each domain offers its own frame of reference and provides its own insight into this communicative phenomenon. While one cannot underestimate the value of these contributions, these various disciplines have tended to establish a tradition of independent scholarship, often isolating themselves from one another. This volume attempts to address this divide and underscores the importance of approaching storytelling from a multidisciplinary perspective. The papers we have included reflect the major themes of: The power of storytelling, testimonial narratives, border and boundaries, mythology, readers' response, and children's narrative. This diversity can only serve to enrich and widen our understanding of storytelling. Through the collective efforts of its contributors, this rich selection of perspectives offers new insights and a lasting contribution to the study of storytelling. The challenge will be for all of us to keep communication between the many disciplines growing.

Irene Maria F. Blayer
Monica Sanchez

Acknowledgments

The most difficult task in finishing any project is making sure that all those deserving of it receive appropriate recognition. Our first thank you must go to the participants of the International Conference on Storytelling 1999, without whose works this volume would not be possible. Second, we would like to thank SSHRC and the Dean of Humanities at Brock University, Dr. John Sivell, for their support. Their sponsorship enabled us to create a collection that we hope will be a welcome contribution to the field of storytelling. Third, we would like to thank Dr. Heidi Burns (senior editor) for walking us through the publication process.

Every task of this magnitude requires social support. We thank our friends, family, and colleagues for their patience with our complaints and for encouraging us when we felt overwhelmed. We must thank Andrew K. Blayer Smith for his smiles, laughter, and love; Dr. Ken Smith for the long hours he spent helping to format the volume and for his unwavering support throughout the completion of the project; Dr. Adolfo Sanchez and Mrs. Eszter Sanchez for their supportive spirit and continual words of encouragement. It is to these four to whom we dedicate this volume.

1

Stones on the Mountain: Crossing Borders into a Story

Kay Stone

As a former geographer, I have an unending fascination with borders and boundaries that surround areas where different elements come together —weather systems, topographical features, countries. I used this geographical concept in my keynote address at the Brock conference, inviting listeners to cross three borders with me—; the border of genre, in this case the genre of the wondertale; the border of transformation within the story; and the personal border into the imagination. I now find that I must add another border, the one between oral and written composition. Because my talk was an oral presentation from an outline rather than a recital of a written essay, translating it into writing has been a challenge. If Marshall McLuhan's overused observation is correct that "the medium is the message," it follows that oral and printed media speak differently. This is something we are aware of as we devote ourselves to narratives and when we make oral presentations. Still, oral and print media are not opposites and in fact have shared their borders and their messages for centuries.

As a folklorist specializing in oral narrative genres, I have been intrigued by the complex interplay between oral and written creativity. This interaction has long been part of folktale tradition. For example, a seventeenth-century collection by Charles Perrault contained seven of his literary compositions based on tales that influenced French readers. Some of these tales were carried orally to Germanic areas by the Huguenots when they fled France at the end of the seventeenth century. A few returned to written form in the Grimm collection, as some of the Grimms' first informants were of Huguenot origin. Many Grimm tales, in turn, found their way back into oral traditions throughout Europe and

North America and other areas as well, distinctive from similar tales already a part of local folklore. For example, one of the stories found in Marie Campbell's collection of Kentucky folktales closely follows the Grimm version of *The Water of Life* (Campbell 183–85), quite distinct from the Catalan variant discussed in this essay.

A fine example of this kind of border crossing comes from twentieth-century Japan. Mrs. Watanabe, a traditional Japanese narrator, turned to printed sources when she began to lose her hearing (Adams 3). Folklorist Robert Adams was surprised to realize that some of the "Japanese" folktales he had collected from her were, in fact, skilful adaptations of Grimm tales that she read (in Japanese) along with Japanese tales in the local school library. She made no distinction between these and her other stories[1] This is an interesting view that will be relevant later, when I retell a Spanish tale that has crossed cultural, linguistic, and media borders.

Let me say a bit more about crossing the border from oral to written stories (and scholarly presentations). When an oral tale is rewritten (that is, recomposed, not simply transcribed), it often becomes more elaborate in description and motivation, as well as in plot and characterization. In contrast, a written story may drop such elaboration when it is taken into oral life. Of course the style and inclination of the author/teller in each case will affect how the story comes to life. I found this to be true when I began to retell a Catalan folktale, *The Water of Life*, which went from oral tradition into a printed collection in Spanish, then into a translated and reworked version by Andrew Lang, and back again into oral form as part of my storytelling repertoire. Much of the literary elaboration of Lang's printed tale disappears quite naturally in the oral telling.

The oral/print border is particularly challenging for a storyteller to cross. If the story begins in print, this can be a triple crossing, from print to oral and back to print. I always find it a challenge to put a told story into written form, as reading is for the eye, and hearing is for the ear. I do not tell a story twice in the same words, even when I have published it in writing. As I learned from tellers I interviewed for my study of storytelling, *Burning Brightly* (Stone 92–238), a told tale is always new, always unfolding again and again as long as it continues to be told. Elsewhere I have discussed the story of *Snow White* and how it was adapted as it crossed borders from oral to print to film[2] The "Disney version" is only one of many.

What I have just said about folktales applies to this essay as well; in oral form it was a relatively informal, conversational presentation based on the loose structure of an outline. I did not explain or describe or elaborate, as I feel compelled to do here, because the needs of a reader are different from those of a hearer.

We come to the place where I am standing now, on the border between oral and written, looking back to see where I have been—my oral keynote address—and forward to where I am now going—into this written essay. I am using the metaphor of a border because it allows me to present my ideas in a more flexible way than if I tried, as I did in the "Snow White" article I mentioned earlier, to set up distinct categories for different kinds of creativity. By using the geographic concept of virtually real borders that circumscribe instead of define, I can create the "Country of Wondertale" and treat it as if we were planning to travel there.

We need to know what preparations are necessary to make this trip successful. Imagine, then, that you are organizing yourself for an actual visit to another country. Does your imaginary border separate distinct places, or does it indicate where they come together? Your view will affect how you interact with the place you visit. This is a matter of attitude because any border separates and unites at the same time. The border that we now stand on lies between the "Country of Wondertale" and the "Country of Reality." Not everyone is comfortable leaving the familiar world of reality. As your guide I can only encourage you to give this a try and see if previous experiences in "Wondertaleland" might be transformed.

Now there is that matter of a passport. A passport identifies your primary connection with where you live and makes this identity clear wherever you travel. This virtual passport relates to how we identify ourselves in professional terms, as linguists, as storytellers, as educators, as literary scholars, and the like. Some are dual citizens, both storyteller and scholar, to suggest one possibility. When your passport is in order, you can decide what sort of visa you wish to travel on. The simplest is the tourist visa, for brief visits with minimal interaction, just to see the sights. Many people visit the Country of Wondertale on tourist visas; for professional storytellers most audiences will be composed of tourists, for example. If you want a more challenging visit you can choose a visa that allows you to stay longer, travel more widely, perhaps even learn the language. If the country proves appealing, you can apply for a work visa (a green card is particularly apt for Wondertale country, where green is the color of magical power). This visa permits you to make return visits as we do when we study a topic or prepare a story for performance.

You might also read a few guidebooks, for example, *Once Upon a Time* (Lüthi), or *Folktales and Society* (Dègh). In them you will learn that the Country of Wondertale is a land in which metaphor is actual; a lion-hearted man might actually be a lion. Within this country we will pass over our second border, one of transformation, which is crossed entirely by chance because it is unmarked. Occasionally there are guardians, like the fox we will meet in *The Water of Life*, but they usually function as helpers, or perhaps as testers, to make certain that you are meant to be on the path. Even when there are guardians, the border is not marked. It might be a forest (as in *The Water of Life*), a river, a wasteland, or an ordinary old well that happens to be the well at the world's end. On the other side of this invisible border, the world will be subtly transformed. Expect the unexpected.

One final suggestion in preparing for this journey is to travel light. This is one trip where you do not need luggage. The less you carry, the more enjoyable it will be. In terms of our professional metaphor, this means that if you can enter this adventure as open-mindedly as possible, you will experience more of its metaphorical and transformative possibilities.

Now we are about to cross into the Country of Wondertale, where there are neither border guards nor customs officials to check your documents, which are for your own orientation. You will see that the inhabitants may look like you and speak your language, but don't be fooled, as they are not ordinary human beings. Some of them are even creatures in disguise.

There are many regions in this land and many neighborhoods in each region. We are traveling to a specific region and neighborhood in search of a story called *The Water of Life*, where we will meet some interesting creatures indeed.

As your tour guide, let me explain a few things about this story. It is one of hundreds, probably thousands, of variants of the basic folktale, though most of these will not have been written down. The few that have been published will be listed in the index of European traditional tales as type number 551 (Aarne-Thompson; Ashliman)[3] Using this number, we can find variant texts in other collections, from as close to the mountains of Kentucky and from as far away as Armenia. Holding to the geographic metaphor, these variants would be found in the same neighborhood, with each house representing a different story and each room a different teller. Some houses would be modest cottages, whereas others would be mansions. The house we are looking for contains a Catalan variant, but we will not meet the teller of the tale because none was identified. We have only the story title and the collector and a story text translated and recomposed in English (Lang 184)[4] Here is a summary of this translation:

A sister and three brothers decide to better their lot by working hard and manage to build both a fine palace and a handsome church. They are told that in order to make these complete, they need to find "a pitcher of the water of life, a branch of the tree . . . whose flowers gives eternal beauty, and the talking bird" (Lang 185). Each brother sets off in turn to find these objects on top of a mountain; each meets a giant who warns them about the speaking stones on the mountain path. All the brothers hear the stones scoffing and mocking, stop to respond, and are turned to stone themselves. The sister now sets off alone on the same path, gets the same advice, and succeeds in walking over the stones, even though "it was as if each stone she stepped on was a living thing" (Lang 188). She reaches the top and finds the three precious things, but as she starts down the path she accidentally drops water on some of the stones, which take their human shape again. She continues downward transforming the stones and returns home with all of the people including her brothers. They plant a branch of the flowering tree, watering it with the magical water, and releasing the talking bird from its cage to settle on the branch. A prince hears of these wonders, comes to see for himself, and falls in love with and marries the sister.

In a small corner of a room in this house we will find another story, the one I am going to tell you. Here the geographic metaphor begins to stretch a bit beyond its capacity to inform. Fit this in, as you will, recalling my earlier comments about oral and written composition and the border between them. Stories pass back and forth over this border with relative ease, culture and language being no hindrance. These crossings alter a story, not only in its adoption to new cultures and languages, but to new tellers as well, as we saw in the case of Mrs. Watanabe in Japan.

In my case, I read the story some time before I told it, hence the changes were even greater than if I had told it immediately after reading it[5] In my oral reconstruction from memory I accurately recalled the magical power of the bird and the flowering tree, how sister and brothers walked over the talking stones to find the water of life, and how the sister transformed the stones on the mountain. However, the order and significance of these motifs had changed as my story evolved, and there were other surprises as well. Somehow a dragon had come into the story, and the prince had left it. After several years of oral telling, the story continued to evolve and adapt, having been taken across the third border to which we will return to shortly, i.e., the ideo-narrative border of personal artistry.

The evolution of stories is further influenced by the covert and overt interactions between tellers and listeners. Face-to-face storytelling at its best is an intimate experience in which tellers and listeners both enter the realm of the story as it unfolds. An effective story can produce a light state of trance, a gentle altered consciousness, for all who take part. Because of this, oral tales never stay quite the same from one telling to the next.

Let us return now to the imaginary house in which the Catalan version of *The Water of Life* exists in order to draw the story out of its corner. Here, then, is the story as I "tell" it in print, somewhat differently from the way I tell it orally[6] It begins in a wasteland.

> Once there was a land so barren that in some places only stones seemed to grow, and only the hardiest trees could survive. A sister and her brothers lived there. They had little between them, but they did have one very precious thing—a tree unlike any other. This tree bloomed just once every year, in the darkest time. It put out one perfect flower on the highest branch, and every year this flower slowly formed a single flawless fruit. On the first day of each New Year when the fruit was ripe, the brothers and sister would take it down, divide it, and eat it. The rest of their year would be filled with joy, which didn't mean they had no sorrows, but only that their troubles did not overwhelm them.
>
> One year everything changed. The tree did not bloom. It had no leaves, no blossoms, no fruit. The sister and her brothers stood at the base of the tree looking up, not knowing what to do. As they watched, a strange and wonderful bird flew out of the clear blue sky and settled on the highest branch. It began to sing a song that entranced them all with the rise and fall of its melody. Beautiful as it was, the sister heard something more, like a soft voice whispering. "Listen!" she said to her brothers. "The bird sings that our tree has stopped blooming because we didn't share the fruit with anyone else." They heard that it would not bloom again unless they found one cup of the Water of Life and brought it to the tree. "Where?" said the older brother, and when he heard that this precious water was in a well on the top of the mountain beyond the great forest, he announced that he would go and find it.
>
> "You all stay here and tend the tree," he said confidently.
>
> "No," said the younger brothers. "We want to go, too."
>
> The sister agreed to stay and care for the tree, but she watched to see which path they took so she might follow if they failed. The three brothers set off together, and she watched them disappear down the long path that led to the great forest.

They walked on and on, further than they'd ever gone in their lives and after some time they came to the forest. There beside the path at the edge of the woods, a red fox crouched, gnawing on a white bone. The fox looked up at them and said politely, "Where are you going and what do you seek?"

"We've come to find the Water of Life," the first brother answered brusquely, "on the top of the mountain beyond this forest."

"I see. But do you know that this is a dangerous road, and that the path up the mountain is even more dangerous? I've never seen anyone come back in all the time I've been here."

"Why" said all the brothers together.

"This is what I know. When your feet touch the stones on the path leading almost to the top of the mountain, those stones will call out. They'll insult you and challenge you and flatter you, and they'll even weep and wail. But anyone who stops to answer the voices becomes one of the stones. They do not return on this path."

The brothers were disturbed to hear this but determined to go on. They hastily thanked the fox and set off into the great dark woods. The path led them through shimmering light and shadowed dark as they walked together. At last they stepped out of the forest into bright sunlight, where they could see a mountain covered with evergreen trees. A narrow path of stones wound up through the cool green woods, almost to the top of the mountain.

"The fox was right," the first brother said eagerly, and he ran to the base of the mountain and began to climb. The very first stone he stepped on spoke to him. "Stop!" it called. He went boldly on, and when he didn't stop, the stones began to insult him. He grew angry as he heard the voices, but he went on. At last their words made him so furious that he forgot the words of the fox and turned to answer them. He stopped. He became one of the stones.

The other two brothers, each in turn, started up the path, and each climbed a little further than the last. But they both suffered the same fate as their brother, the second giving in to the voices that challenged, and the third to those that flattered. None of them came back down the fox's path.

The sister waited at home for some time until she was sure that her brothers were not going to return. She prepared herself and then set off on the path her brothers had taken. She too met the fox, who asked:

"Where are you going and what do you seek?"

She answered the fox politely and listened thoughtfully to what the fox said in response. She learned that the long path was dangerous, that anyone who stopped would become one of stones. She guessed what must have become of her brothers. She thanked the fox, said goodbye, and went on her way.

She passed through the great forest of shimmering light and shadowed dark. At last she came out into the open and saw the mountain and its stony path. She walked toward the mountain, and soon enough she came to the first stone of the path and heard it call out "stop!" She struggled on up the winding path, listening to the angry voices of the stones beneath her feet. Each stone called out insults, and then challenges, and at last they began to flatter her.

"Do stop!" they called in sweet voices, "You're a remarkable woman to have come this far. Stop and share your secret with us." She was tempted to help, but even when she heard her last brother's voice among them she went on, sorry that she was now completely alone. Then the stones began to wail and to cry out in pitiful voices:

"Oh please! Stop! Stop! Please don't leave us here like this, all alone. We've been lying here for so long, so very long."

She heard their anguished voices and now she really wanted to stop and help them, but she remembered the fox's words. If she stopped now she would become one of them, unable to help at all. In tears, she willed her feet to move over the weeping stones one step at a time, up and up, with their sad voices calling out behind her as she went on.

The way grew steeper and more difficult, but she continued to climb, remembering the fox's words as she went. Finally the path ended and she found herself at the top of the mountain, with the world spread out below. At her feet lay an ancient well, and on the edge of the well was a small silver cup. She reached down to pick up the cup, but as her fingers touched it she heard a deep hissing sound. The earth under her feet began to tremble and shake, then the well was filled with a deep roaring like the sound of a fierce storm approaching. She stood there watching, and before her startled eyes the head and neck of a great golden dragon rose up slowly from the well until it towered above her. The dragon spoke in a voice filled with rolling thunder:

"Where you are going and what do you seek?"

"I've come for the Water of Life," she stammered, "just one cup, for the tree."

"One cup, you say? That is much more than you think. But I will allow you to take one cup . . . if you do something for me."

"What could I do for you?" she said, her voice full of fear.

"You can polish the scales on the top of my head until each one glows like the sun. If you do that, you may take one cup of the Water of Life."

She looked at her ordinary hands, and, with nothing else to offer, she agreed. The dragon bent down his great golden head, and she began to polish the scales, each one carefully. When she finished, he lifted his great head and hissed slowly, carefully,

"One cup is yours. Take care how you use it."

As the golden dragon sank back down, the well filled with surging water. She seized the silver cup and filled it, turned quickly, and started back down the mountain.

When she came to the first stone she tripped, and one drop of water fell from the cup onto the stone. Before her eyes that stone turned into a human being. They looked at each other in amazement, and then she looked at the water in the cup. She touched the next stone with the water. This stone, too, became a human being. And the next . . . And the next . . . And the next.

She noticed that the water in the cup did not diminish, and then she understood the dragon's words. One cup was much more. She moved down the path touching each of the stones with one drop of precious water and watched as each stone took its own human shape again. Happiest of all to see her were her own brothers. The four of them together, followed by all the people who had been stones, carried the cup back to the tree.

The people gathered in a great circle and watched as the four poured out the precious water at the base of the tree, and as it sank slowly into the earth the tree began to put out new leaves, then blossoms. As they watched, each blossom turned into perfect fruit, exactly enough for all who were there. The sister and brothers divided all the fruit and shared it with every person there. Each who tasted it found that their New Year was filled with joy, which didn't mean they had no sorrows, only that their troubles did not overwhelm them. Because they did that, the tree never stopped blooming again. Trees began to grow in that stony land once more, but only one tree bore the fruit of joy.

So it was, and ever will be, even now to this very day.

Now I invite you to leave behind the Country of Wondertale by providing a bridge that connects us with the Country of Real. This bridge is a fanciful closing formula that sometimes appears at the end of Russian folktales, using the device of a fictional narrator who has been "present" in the story:

There was a great feast, and I was there.

But not one drop could I drink, nor one bite could I eat.

They gave me socks made of white milk and boots made of paper.

On my way here I fell in a puddle and they were all washed away.

So I come here to you now with only the story.

As the actual and not the fictional narrator, I assure you that I was, in fact, present in the story as I told it, and that those who listened also had this possibility. This brings us to the final border that surrounds your own "country," that of your imagination. We all have the capacity for being present in a story at its most effective moments, when our imagination is fully engaged. However, no matter how entranced we might become, eventually the story must be left behind as we return to our ordinary reality. When leaving somewhere after a visit, it is traditional practice to take home souvenirs of the trip, ones that cannot be washed away in a puddle.

This is where my geographic metaphor begins to stretch a bit far; we cannot bring back anything material from our virtual visit—no snapshots of the dragon, no miniature silver cups engraved with the words *Water of Life*, no pet rocks with foxes painted on them7 However, if we consider the French meaning of souvenir, "to remember," there are many imaginative possibilities. For example, you can allow a moment of a story to come back to you: an image, a sound, a feeling, and a movement. In describing this silently or aloud, the heart of the story becomes visible.

Or you can imagine yourself inside the story as it was when you heard it or just now as you read it. Notice where you were in relation to the action. Was it happening in front of you, like a movie or a theatrical production, or was it moving around you, as if you were walking through a movie or a play? Were you viewing the action from ground level or from above (and at what height)? Can you see any of the characters walking and guess from how they move what kind of person they might be? Any of these remembered moments aid you in recalling the core of the story in your words through your remembered souvenirs. In doing so, you have made your own border crossing, passing into a place that I cannot enter, your own room in the house where the story can now live.

When I told *The Water of Life* at the conference, the participants were in the same place at the same time, but now we are scattered in place and time and have crossed this border into the printed word. Many of you who were not present have only this written account of the event, so your experience might be like watching slides of a friend's trip to Europe. This essay itself now becomes a souvenir.

Using the concept of geographic borders allowed me to surround wondertales with an imaginative boundary instead of defining them in a linear way. This has permitted us to conceive of narratives as actual places to visit, and I have suggested ways to bring back mental souvenirs of our adventures. My hope was to expand the experience from an intellectual exercise into virtual reality. If I have been an effective tour guide, the story of *The Water of Life*, its characters, and its exploits are not separate, not "out there" safely removed from us. A told story ideally offers this kind of immediate experience. My written account is a recreation of the experience, a record of the event for those who were present at the initial telling. However, it also stands on its own here. As active readers, your immediate memories, your own souvenirs, allow you to cross the oral/written border and recreate the story for yourselves, making it more than a mere record.

My hope is that the concept of geographic borders and what is needed to cross them offer a practical approach into narratives. We enter other worlds on many levels when exploring stories as tellers and as scholars. We do so with the conscious and unconscious perception that we cross borders carrying a firm identity—a passport—with our work, and with a specific intent—a visa—for how long and how deep our interaction will be.

Notes

1. This was the case with a Cree narrator, Nathaniel Queskekapow, as well. He told a brief fable in my folklore class that turned out to be his original reworking of Chicken Little. He did not introduce it as a European tale; for him it was, quite simply, a Cree tale, now part of his rich repertoire. Those of us accustomed to written, authored literature with an unchanging text might find this kind of "appropriation" difficult to understand, but it is not difficult at all for narrators who grew up surrounded by oral tradition.
2. "Three Transformations of Snow White," in The Brothers Grimm and the Folktale (McGlathery 52–65).
3. The Aarne-Thompson tale type index is an invaluable tool for anyone doing comparative work on folktales from Indo-European tradition, as it summarizes a basic tale and provides a type number that allows readers to search other collections for variant texts. Ashliman's very useful index, based on Aarne-Thompson, lists current books that contain published texts. For The Quest for the Water of Life, he identifies 21 sources, including stories from Germany, Russia, Romania, Scotland, England, Ireland, Italy, Norway, Armenia, Greece, Ecuador, and from Kentucky's Appalachian Mountains.
4. Lang identified his source as Cuentos Populars Catalans, Dr. D. Francisco de S. Maspous y Labros, Barcelona, 1885.
5. Part of this discussion appears in a previous article on this story, though my emphasis is quite different (Stone "Fire," 139–44). The article describes the oral evolution of The Water of Life in greater detail and has a different focus from the one this essay has.
6. This text is a reworking of a printed version I contributed to a collection of Canadian folktales (Yashinsky) with additional slight changes for this writing. A variant text can be found in an article in the storytelling journal, Marvels & Tales (Stone 139–44). As I said earlier, an oral story never quite stays the same, even in writing.
7. In fact, I do have a stone like that, painted by a student who was very fond of the fox in The Water of Life. Of course, the stone does not come directly from the story itself but from her own imagination. In such a way, a memory can become a concrete souvenir—as a painting, a poem, a dance.

Works Cited

Aarne, Antti, and Stith Thompson. *The Types of the Folktale: A Classification and Bibliography.* Folklore Fellows Communications No. 84. Helsinki: Academia Scientiarum Fennica, 1973.

Adams, Robert. "Social Identity of a Japanese Storyteller." Diss. Indiana University, 1972.

Ashliman, D. L. *A Guide to Folktales in the English Language.* Westport, CT: Greenwood Press, 1987.

Campbell, Marie. *Tales From the Cloud Walking Country.* 1958. Westport, CT: Greenwood Press, 1976.

Dègh, Linda. *Folktales and Society: Storytelling in a Hungarian Community.* Bloomington: Indiana University Press, 1989.

Lang, Andrew. *The Pink Fairy Book.* 1897. New York: Dover, 1967.

Lüthi, Max. *Once Upon a Time.* Bloomington: Indiana University Press, 1976.

McGlathery, James. *The Brothers Grimm and the Folktale.* Urbana: University of Illinois Press, 1988.

Perrault, Charles. *Perrault's Complete Fairy Tales.* Trans. A. E. Johnson and others. New York: Dodd, Mead, 1961.

Stone, Kay. *Burning Brightly: New Light on Old Tales Told Today.* Peterborough, Ontario: Broadview Press, 1998.

———. "Fire and Water: A Journey into the Heart of a Story." *Marvels & Tales: Journal of Fairy-Tale Studies* 14.1 (2000):139–44.

Yashinsky, Dan. *At The Edge: A Book of Canadian Stories.* Charlottetown, Prince Edward Island: Ragweed Press, 1998.

2

Lost in a Story:
Modeling Storytelling and Storylistening

Brian W. Sturm

"Far-li-mas, today the day has arrived when you must cheer me. Tell me a story." "The performance is quicker than the command," said Far-li-mas, and began. The king and his guests forgot to drink, forgot to breathe. The slaves forgot to serve. They, too, forgot to breathe. For the art of Far-li-mas was like hashish, and, when he had ended, all were as though enveloped in a delightful swoon. The king had forgotten his thoughts of death. Nor had any realized that they were being held from twilight until dawn; but when the guests departed they found the sun in the sky

—Joseph, Campbell, *The Legend of the Destruction of Kash*

On that day, the reciter was enchanting the audience with the story of Hanuman the monkey and how he had to leap across the ocean to take Rama's signet ring to Sita, the abducted wife of Rama. When Hanuman was making his leap, the signet ring slipped from his hand and fell into the ocean. Hanuman didn't know what to do. He had to get the ring back quickly and take it to Sita in the demon's kingdom. While he was wringing his hands, the husband, who was listening with rapt attention in the first row, said, "Hanuman, don't worry. I'll get it for you." Then he jumped up and dived into the ocean, found the ring in the ocean floor, and brought it back and gave it to Hanuman.

—A. K. Ramanujan, *What Happens When You Really Listen*

Storytelling in the United States has enjoyed a renaissance in the past twenty years. Books on how to select, prepare, and present stories fill the bookstores' shelves, and professional storytellers make careers performing stories at festivals, libraries, schools, and conferences throughout the nation. Whereas researchers have studied story from many perspectives, one element of storytelling has remained nearly unconsidered, and it is, perhaps, the most profound and influential characteristic of storytelling: its power to entrance those who listen. As the excerpts from the stories above show, people who listen to stories can undergo a profound change in their experience of reality. The normal, waking state of consciousness changes as the story takes on a new dimension. Listeners seem to experience the story with remarkable immediacy, engaging in the story's plot and with the story's characters, and they may enter an altered state of consciousness. What is this phenomenon, and what does the listener experience during this altered state? Is it qualitatively different from a person's normal state of consciousness and in what ways? What influences the listener's ability to experience this altered state? These are the questions this essay addresses to build a phenomenologically rich description of the listener's experience of the entrancing power of storytelling.

Conceptual Framework

The conceptual framework for this study is influenced by the theoretical principles of multiple disciplines, including psychology, cognitive science, literary philosophy, communication, folklore, rhetorical studies, linguistics, medicine, counseling, hypnosis, and religious studies. The principal elements, however, can be traced to the theories of reader response criticism, consciousness and its states, and systems theory.

Louise Rosenblatt, a prominent reader response theoretician, discusses the need in literary philosophy and literary criticism to study the impact of a text on its reader. She draws a useful distinction between a text and a poem, claiming that the text is what the author creates, while the true poem is what the reader creates, using the text as the foundation and adding to it her personal associations, experiences, images, memories, expectations, perceptions, and the like. "The poem [is] the experience shaped by the reader under the guidance of the text" (12). This concept is applicable to the storytelling event. The storyteller recounts the text, while the listeners create the true story based on the verbal text and overlaid with personal images and memories. Whereas there is a continual feedback loop present in any storytelling event—as the teller changes the story to accommodate the audience—the unit of study, following Rosenblatt's thesis, is more each listener's experience than the storyteller's performance.

Research of consciousness has taken diverse perspectives. Structuralists have concentrated on describing the elements of consciousness, the discrete units that may compose it (see Marsh; Csikszentmihalyi;

Battista). Functionalists have emphasized the significance of psychological processes to the ongoing development of the individual and his or her role in society (see Stephen), while behaviorists claim either that consciousness should not be the focus of psychological inquiry at all because it is not an external, perceptible behavior (see Watson), or that it should be linked to physiological events (see Boring). Finally, the constructivist notion that organisms construct the universe in which they live based on cultural, environmental, and personal perceptions has reinvigorated the study of consciousness.

Systems theory, and holistic thinking in general, has become popular in the last thirty years, and it is being productively applied to many areas of research. It arose as a reaction to the mechanistic paradigm (the dominant paradigm based in seventeenth-century physics), which views nature as inert, truth as value free, cause and effect as basically linear, and consciousness as epiphenomenal—the behaviorists' position that mental processes are simply secondary phenomena resulting from neural processes in the brain (see Berman). Systems theorists, on the other hand, view nature as an organism (Lovelock's "Gaia hypothesis"), a system of interacting elements, the sum of which is greater than the parts. They believe that truth is value laden, cause and effect are interactive, and consciousness is constructed and more than a simple reflection of neural energy.

Charles T. Tart has developed a systems approach to states of consciousness. "While the components of consciousness can be studied in isolation, they exist as parts of a complex system, consciousness, and can be fully understood only when we see this function in the overall system" (Tart 3). He posits the existence of a basic awareness in all humans, which, when it comes under volitional control, is called "attention." He also claims that certain structures exist that are "relatively permanent structures/functions/subsystems of the mind/brain that act on information to transform it in various ways" (Tart 4). A person's "discrete state of consciousness," the "unique, dynamic pattern or configuration of psychological structures" (Tart 5), can be considered the system of psychological structures that have been activated by attention/awareness, and that are interacting at any particular time.

The discrete state of consciousness to which most people are accustomed is the one in which they spend the majority of their waking lives. This can be considered the "baseline state of consciousness," and any major deviation from this baseline is considered a "discrete altered state of consciousness." When something happens to destabilize the baseline

(Tart's "disruptive forces"), consciousness proceeds through a "transitional period" in which the psychological structures of consciousness are reshuffled, and an altered state may result, though this is not necessarily the outcome of such a psychological shake-up. There are many "stabilizing forces" involved that work to solidify any discrete state of consciousness, especially the baseline one (if there were not, we would all be slipping between discrete states of consciousness without any conception of one being primary or normal). Once the baseline is made unstable, the resulting disarray of psychological structures must be reconstituted into a new system (with the help of Tart's "patterning forces"). The new system will include some of the structures of the baseline state of consciousness, some new structures, and a new design, or interaction, of these structures (see Tart 73, for his model of this process).

Methodological Issues

There is concern among some researchers that reported personal experience is not a viable source of data. This concern stems mainly from the behaviorists' perception that behaviors are public and can be validated by outside observers, whereas introspective accounts are private and hence not subject to external corroboration. Kukla ("Toward a Science of Experience"), however, claims that the public/private distinction of earlier researchers is untenable. If we cannot prove the validity of an introspective report, neither can we *prove* the validity of an observer's subjective report. Pekala summarizes the issue:

> Although phenomenological observations may be more difficult to verify than most behavioral observations, they are not unverifiable. Repeated observations by the same subject, observations of many subjects in reference to the phenomena of interest, observations tied to verifiable and repeatable stimulus conditions, and correlation of introspective observations with behavioral, physiological, and/or neurochemical data can all lead to increased verification, as can experimental and statistical control of subject characteristics and training. (28–29)

There is also a concern that lived experience differs dramatically from reported experience. This issue parallels the current belief that memory cannot purely recreate experience; instead a remembered experience is an amalgam of the lived experience and other memories and associations. There is, in this study, an inherent assumption that the reported experience is sufficiently close to the lived one to warrant evaluation; interviewing as a data collection methodology relies on this very assumption.

I recruited twenty-two participants from eight Midwest storytelling festivals to interview. Each interview took place immediately after the storytelling to decrease the memory decay due to passing time (Thompson), to keep memory as unconsidered as possible (Ericsson), and to keep the context of memory retrieval similar to the context of memory encoding, which aids in recall (see Begg and White). I approached listeners who seemed interested in the storytelling (i.e., they were basically paying attention), but who did not necessarily show precise physiological evidence of a discrete altered state of consciousness. This approach helped broaden the descriptive base of the study, and it provided information on what hinders entry into this discrete altered state of consciousness. To get a variety of experiential data, I interviewed people ranging in age from childhood (at least eight years old) to the elderly; no attempt was made to use age as a variable because the focus of this study was on one holistic picture, not on individual or group differences. Each interview was audiotape recorded, transcribed, sent to the participant for review, and finally coded for emergent categories.

Results

My analysis of the interviews and participant-observation data, combined with other researchers' efforts to model storytelling, has helped me create two models of the storylistening experience. The first model (figure 1) describes the storylistening experience, whereas the second (figure 2) concentrates on the storylistening trance.

The storytelling experience begins with the section labeled number one: the point of conversation before a story is brought up. The teller is labeled as such solely to distinguish her representation in the diagram from those of the listeners. At this stage, however, all those involved in conversation are on an equal footing. No one has been granted an extended turn at speaking, and all interact equally. On the level of consciousness, this stage corresponds with the listener's normal, waking consciousness that usually involves constant reality checking, active data processing, and attentive awareness.

In stage two, the teller brings up the idea of a story, thereby bringing it into existence. The story is still an external entity, not yet shared but anticipated by all. The teller introduces the story, gives it a boundary, and sets it off as something different and special. She announces, in effect, that "What follows is no longer ordinary conversation, and it deserves your undivided attention." As the listeners begin to bring their attention to focus on the teller (not the story since it has not yet been broached), a bond is formed between them; a bond signified by the overlapping symbols in the diagram.

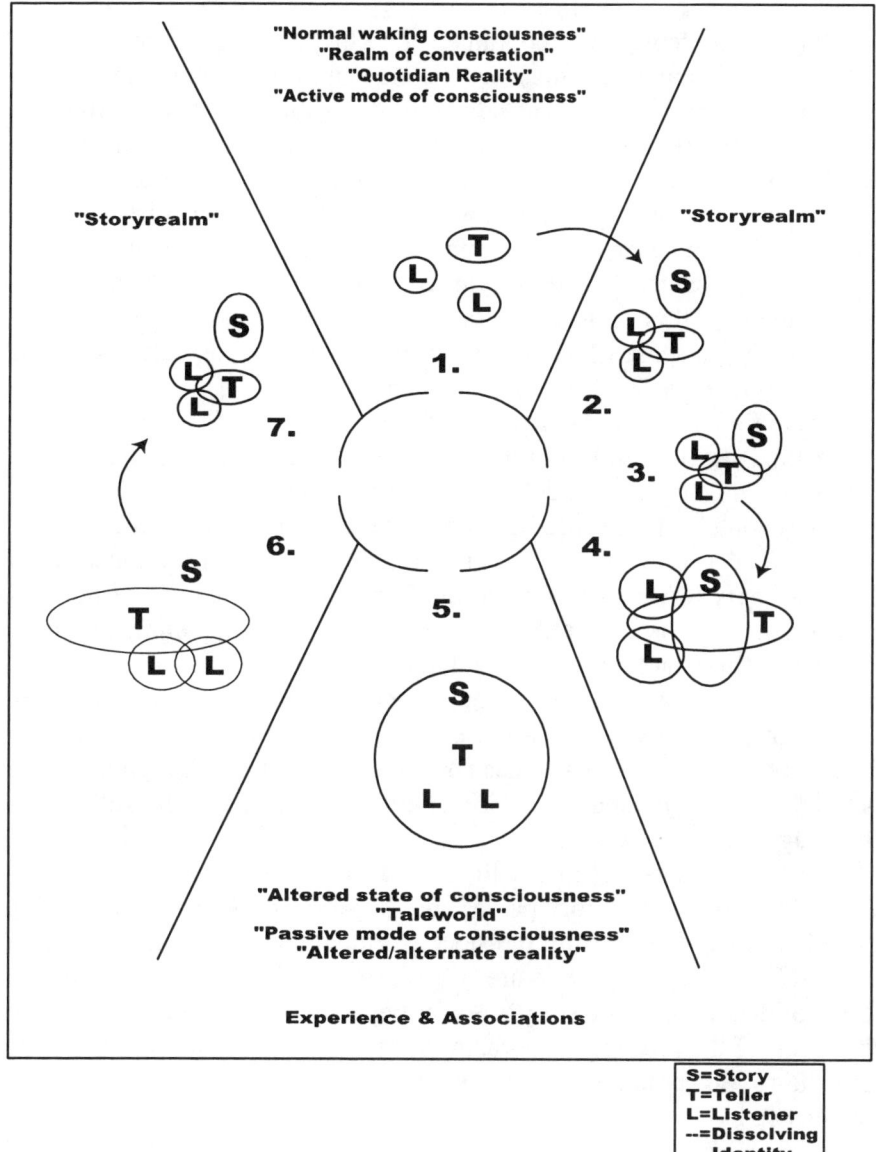

Figure 1. Storylistening Experience Model

In stage three, the listeners and the teller draw ever more together, melding the bond necessary for the arrival of the story. The storyteller begins to enter the story. She plays with it, beginning to form the mental images that she will portray to the listeners. She forms a bond with the story, and it begins to engross her.

Stage four depicts the continued growth of the bond between the teller and the listeners. As the story begins to unfold in telling, it captures the minds of the listeners and begins to draw them in. It has grown in size as its importance in the event increases. Soon it will dominate the event and those involved. There is also a developing sense of the communal nature of the experience, and a bond begins to form between the listeners. Each listener is engaged in creating his or her own story based on the text presented by the storyteller, and, although each of these stories is unique, all are interrelated and influenced by the ongoing experience. There is a sense of a cocreated experience in which each listener is involved (Georges "Toward an Understanding of").

Stage five is the climactic one of the altered state of consciousness. It is the time in the telling during which the listeners and the teller lose themselves in the story and live its reality. Quotidian reality is nearby, and occasionally it "invades" the listener's awareness and brings him or her out of reverie with a start, but it largely remains on the outskirts of consciousness (the reason for the open spaces in the center of the diagram). Attention is centered in the story. The lines depicting the teller and the listeners are broken and intertwined as their roles and identities merge with the personae in the story (which may or may not happen). The listener's reality becomes more relative as the story takes on its own kind of reality. The teller still has control over the story, though often she is also caught up in an altered state of consciousness, and she still guides the imagery of the listeners.

As the climax—not in the literary sense but in the sense of altered consciousness—of the story passes and the story winds down (stage six), the teller emerges first from the story world enough to begin the process of bringing the listeners, who are still engrossed in the story, back toward the quotidian realm. The story's power begins to fade, and it moves from the realm of the present to the realm of the past and memory. The dotted line shows the breaking up of the boundaries that have held the story together.

In stage seven, as in stage two, the teller maintains her link with the listeners as they all withdraw from the story. This is often the time for closing formulae that show the listeners that the story has passed and that it is time to reenter the realm of the quotidian. The "space" created by the story dissolves, the teller holds on to the listeners a moment longer to be sure they have come out of the story, and then they all return to the quotidian realm of conversation (stage one). The entire storytelling event is enclosed in a boundary of experience and associations. It is within the bounds of, and in connection with, our experience that a story makes sense, and our associations with the story give it power.

The particular area of interest for this article is stage five, and the interviews indicate that people often do experience a qualitatively different state of consciousness while listening to stories. The participants mentioned six characteristics of this trance state:

1. Realism ("it's not flat like TV; it's real," "it's the actual living of the images")
2. Lack of awareness of surroundings ("I can completely forget about everything else except the story," "everything else around you just blacks out," "I just kind of fall into a different world")
3. Engaged receptive channels (visual: "I was making pictures in my mind," "it was so powerfully presented and evoked so many images . . . [that] it's like watching a movie or a play"; auditory: "I don't see any pictures; I listen to the words," "I can just hear her voice on the tape, and I can be transported"; kinesthetic: "there are physical changes that happen while you're listening," "if it's really good and you really relate, your pulse goes up"; and emotional: "I respond emotionally to the stories," "they'd [the storyteller] get excited, and so I would get excited")
4. Lack or loss of control of the experience ("the visions that *she brings to me*," "his vivid descriptions *made you feel* like you were really there," "a couple of tellers would *get you* into it more than others")
5. "Placeness," a spatial reference often referred to as "in" or "there" ("I feel I'm inside the story . . . I'm sitting there totally in the story," "It's like I'm really there sometimes")
6. Time distortion—the lengthening or shortening of a person's subjective perception of time ("time goes pretty quickly usually when you're in the story; you get into it, and then it's over," "the story seemed longer, because it just gets you into it, and it seems longer to me that way")

There are many influences on a listener's state of consciousness during a storytelling event that may either increase or decrease the likelihood of a trance state occurring. These influences differ from the characteristics of the storylistening trance mentioned earlier in that they tend to trigger or inhibit the trance experience rather than describe it. The listeners whom I interviewed mentioned a variety of positive influences, including: the storytelling style, the activation of the listener's memories, the listener's feeling of safety or comfort (both physical and emotional), the story content, the storyteller's ability, the storyteller's involvement in the story, the listener's expectations being met, the listener's personal preferences being matched, the listener's occupation or training, the sense of a rapport between the listener and the storyteller, the novelty or familiarity of the story, rhythm, humor, and recency. They also mentioned negative influences that can be grouped under the heading of "distractions." Figure 2 is a diagram of one possible system of interaction of these influences that is meant to be exploratory rather than prescriptive.

The model is composed of three concentric circles representing the baseline state of consciousness, the transitional period, and the discrete altered state of consciousness (termed d-ASCin figure 2), respectively. The breadth of each circle is misleading (but prescribed by the typeface of the letters); the baseline would certainly be the largest one, both in size and volume, since people spend the majority of their lives there. The transitional period, for the storylistening trance experience, would best be displayed as very thin; it lasts moments, minutes at the longest. The trance itself would remain its current size; I believe this model aptly represents the extent of the trance.

The spokes of the wheel, as it were, are portals or conduits from the baseline to the altered state of consciousness and are represented in the diagram as tubes. Each conduit is equipped with a valve at the end that touches the baseline state of consciousness. This valve is generally about half open during normal consciousness, and it represents the ease with which consciousness can slip from one state to the altered state. If the valve is wide open, the conduit becomes readily accessible; if it is entirely closed, then that avenue of access to the altered state is blocked. The conduits, themselves, are labeled with the influences that the research participants identified. There are certainly others that I have not included because they did not surface during the interviews. For example, one of the characteristics of the story listening trance is time distortion. I believe this characteristic can also serve as an influence; as a listener notices a change in his concept of time passing, the effect and the trance may intensify. Time distortion, then, could also be represented as a conduit in this diagram (for that matter, it could also act as a distraction if it frightened you enough to break apart your trance state and reconstitute the baseline). I make no claim that these, and only these, conduits exist.

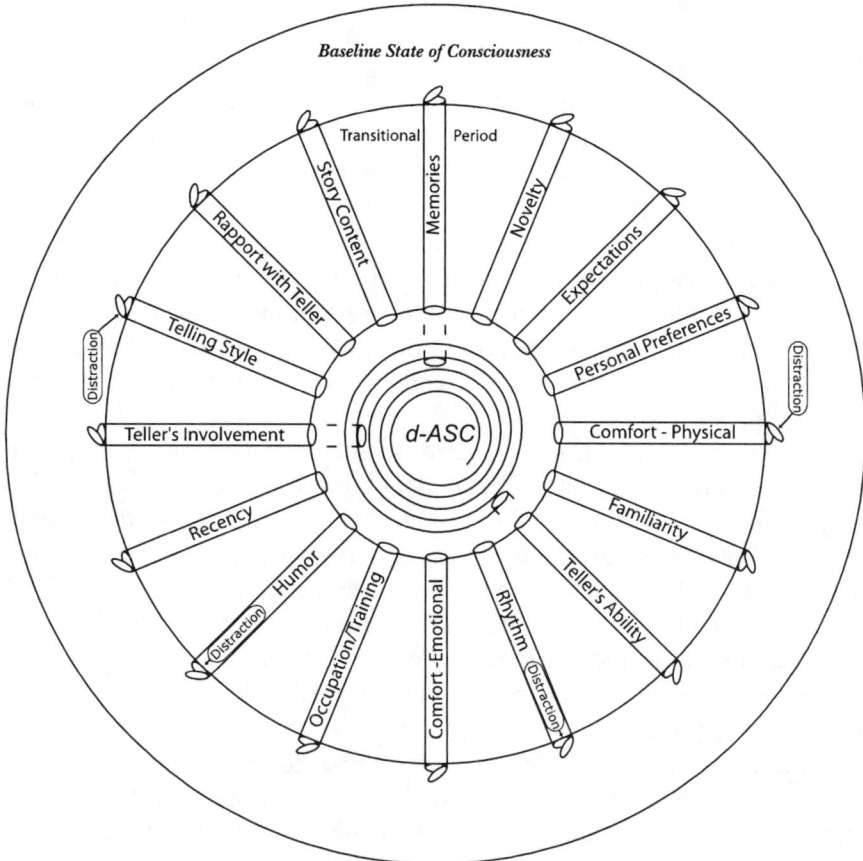

Figure 2. Storylistening Trance Model

Distractions (of which there are four in the diagram, but of which there are many in reality) provide the impetus either to close the valves on the conduits if they occur while a person is in the baseline state of consciousness or to open those valves if the distractions occur while a person is in an altered state and hence the force is shown on either side of the valves. Distractions can open or close the valve on any conduit, and one powerful distraction may affect all of them simultaneously. In short, a shift in consciousness is enabled by open conduits and hindered by closed ones. These valves can also be influenced by individual differences. For example, some people may never be swayed by rhythm; for them, rhythm is not a conduit to trance. For others, rhythm may be an essential and readily available conduit.

I believe there is a distractibility threshold below which a distraction is outweighed by a listener's involvement and is not noticed. This threshold is not visually represented, but it plays a role in the force needed to open or close the conduit valves. In other words, a slight distraction that occurs while a listener is in the baseline state of consciousness may not be strong enough to close the valves on any conduit, and so the person's consciousness does not register it and is still able to access the altered state. If the person is already in the altered state and a slight distraction arises, this distraction may not be sufficient to open the conduit valves and allow (or force) the person's consciousness to escape the trance. The person in normal consciousness can still enter the altered state in spite of the distraction, just as the person in the trance can remain there despite it.

The listener's attention or awareness energy is not represented by a location or a name as it is in Tart's model, but it is nevertheless present. This energy flows through the baseline, the conduits, and the altered state. It flows when caught up in a story, through the conduits into the region of the altered state. There is, however, nothing that requires all of this energy to flow through the conduits; some of it might remain in the baseline to monitor the world (i.e., a car driver who becomes lost in listening to a book on tape but remains on the road). This being true, a person could very easily be in multiple states of consciousness at any moment: Some of his or her awareness would be flowing through the baseline state; some might be traversing to an altered state, and still more might be within the altered state. This perspective belies the exclusive nature of "this or that" and enables multiple awarenesses. Perhaps researchers should speak of "attentions" and "awarenesses" in the plural rather than the singular and see whether this opens up new insights.

At the center of the discrete altered state of consciousness area (d-ASC) is a spiral with only a few of the conduits penetrating its sides. This spiral represents the depth of the altered state of consciousness. As a person goes deeper and deeper into trance (around the spiral), the conduits become harder to access. Some conduits, not necessarily the ones diagrammed here, may be able to reach deeper into the trance state, allowing the person a chance to exit; however, at the deepest levels of an altered state, egress can become difficult, if not impossible (in extreme psychosis, for example), but this rarely happens. There is no evidence, either in this research or in the literature that I have examined, that a person can go so deeply into the storylistening trance that the experience becomes a psychotic episode.

The participants of this study confirm the existence of a qualitatively different state of consciousness that accompanies some experiences of listening to stories. They describe several characteristics of the storylistening trance and enumerate multiple influences on their normal conscious state that can trigger or hinder the ensuing trance-like state. I have proposed two models that I hope will stimulate conversation about this phenomenon and lead to further research into the storylistening trance.

Works Cited

Battista, John R. "The Science of Consciousness." *The Stream of Consciousness: Scientific Investigations into the Flow of Human Experience.* Ed. K. S. Pope and J. L. Singer. New York: Plenum Press, 1978. 55–90.
Begg, Ian, and Pamela White. "Encoding Specificity in Interpersonal Communication." *Journal of Verbal Learning and Verbal Behavior* 21 (1982): 70–87.
Berman, Morris. "The Shadow Side of Systems Theory." *Journal of Humanistic Psychology* 36 (1996): 28–54.
Boring, Edwin G. *The Physical Dimensions of Consciousness.* New York: Dover, 1963.
Campbell, Joseph. *The Masks of God: Primitive Mythology.* New York: Penguin, 1969.
Csikszentmihalyi, Mihalyi. *Flow: The Psychology of Optimal Experience.* New York: Harper and Row, 1990.
Ericsson, K. Anders, and Herbert Simon. "Verbal Reports as Data." *Psychological Review* 87 (1980): 215–51.
Georges, Robert. "Toward an Understanding of Storytelling Events." *Journal of American Folklore* 82 (1969): 313–28.
Kukla, Andre. "Toward a Science of Experience." *Journal of Mind and Behavior* 4 (1983): 231–46.
Lovelock, James E. *Gaia: A New Look at Life on Earth.* Oxford: Oxford University Press, 1979.
Marsh, Caryl A. "A Framework for Describing Subjective States of Consciousness." *Alternate States of Consciousness.* Ed. N. E. Zinberg. New York: Free Press, 1977. 121–44.
Pekala, Ronald J. *Quantifying Consciousness: An Empirical Approach.* New York: Plenum Press, 1991.
Ramanujan, A. K. *Folktales from India: A Selection of Oral Tales from Twenty-Two Languages.* New York: Pantheon Books, 1991.
Rosenblatt, Louise M. *The Reader, the Text, the Poem: The Transactional Theory of the Literary Work.* Carbondale: Southern Illinois University Press, 1978.
Stephen, Michele. "Dreams of Change: The Innovative Role of Altered States of Consciousness in Traditional Melanesian Religion." *Oceania* 1 (1979): 3–22.
Tart, Charles T. *States of Consciousness.* New York: Dutton, 1975.
Thompson, Charles P. "Memory for Unique Personal Events: The Roommate Study." *Memory and Cognition* 10 (1982): 324–32.
Watson, John B. "Psychology as the Behaviorist Views It." *Psychological Review* 20 (1913): 158.

3

Tracking the Limits of Interpretation: A Reading of the Novels of Umberto Eco

Corrado Federici

Umberto Eco (b. 1932-) is a prolific theoretician, literary critic, popular culture essayist, and novelist who perhaps is best known for his medieval detective story, *The Name of the Rose*. In all of these domains, which inform each other, he has been primarily interested in investigating the process of interpretation: How it comes about; what roles are played by the author, the text, and the reader, and what the properties of meaning are. A consistent concern of his has been the delicate balance between the reader's freedom to interpret a text according to his or her personal preferences and the restrictions imposed on that freedom by the code in which the text is written as well as by other cultural factors.

As a professor of semiotics at the University of Bologna, Italy, Eco has been a prominent international figure in the development of the science of signs, that is to say, the study of the nature of communication by means of symbols. His seminal work in this area is *A Theory of Semiotics*, published in 1976, in which his theories are born out of a dialogue with the ideas of linguists such as Ferdinand de Saussure (1857–1913) and philosophers such as Charles Saunders Peirce (1839–1914). Of crucial importance in the transmission of information through any code is the process of interpretation of the symbol and the relationship between the symbol and the object that it represents. Eco's interest in the complexities of this topic continues throughout his career and assumes many forms. The strictly semiotic dimension of his inquiry has led to the publication of the very substantial work, *Semiotics and the Philosophy of Language* (1984). One of the issues that must be confronted by those who examine the nature of the sign is that of the multiple meanings conveyed by a symbol (polysemy). Stated differently, theorists must not only account for the mechanisms that produce a specific meaning; they must also account for all the possible meanings a given term can evoke in the individual to whom the message is directed, as well as the mechanism that either encourages or discourages an infinite number of interpretations of the sign.

However, Eco also examines the interpretative process in the context of literary works in which, of course, every word is a sign that must be decoded. In his *Opera aperta* of 1962 (translated as *The Open Work* in 1989), the author reflects on the differences between a "closed" piece of writing, which more or less controls the reader's response, and an "open" text, which is deliberately constructed so as to invite multiple interpretations. "However, while it abstains from 'validating' any one interpretation, it [the open text] conditions and limits all possible readings" (Francese 158). The examination of the strategies used by a writer to create such an "open" work, in turn, has led Eco to consider more directly the participation of the reader of the text in the entire process of meaning-making and produced works such as *The Role of the Reader* (1979) and *Six Walks in the Fictional Woods* (1994).

Convinced that his readers considered him to be advocating the validity of every conceivable interpretation of a given text, Eco decided to address the question of the explicit constraints that exist in the text, which permit certain readings and invalidate or disallow others. In this vein, he wrote *The Limits of Interpretation* (1990), *Interpretation and Overinterpretation* (1992) and *Misreadings* (1993). For critics, Umberto Eco, "now also wants a 'reader-oriented' theory to realize that readers cannot escape submitting to some constraints in general" (Tejera 147). In formulating his ideas on the nature of those constraints, Eco states that there are,

> two ideas of interpretation. On the one side it is assumed that to interpret a text means to find out the meaning intended by its original author or . . . its objective nature or essence. . . . On the other side it is assumed that texts can be interpreted in infinite ways. Taken as such, these two opinions are both instances of epistemological fanaticism. (henceforth *The Limits* 25)

The author establishes as the poles of his dialectic or discourse, what he refers to as "hermetic drift" and "deconstructionist free play." He first advocates the primacy of one particular or correct interpretation of a given text. Eco himself provides a working definition of this expression saying:

> I shall call Hermetic drift the interpretive habit which dominated Renaissance Hermeticism and which is based on the principle of universal analogy and sympathy according to which every item of furniture of the world is linked to every other element (or to many) of this world and to every element (or many) of the superior world by means of similitudes and resemblances. (*The Limits* 24)

The other extreme position suggests that no interpretation is ultimately valid because "Deconstruction . . . negates any intrinsic meaning of the text and locates meaning only outside it, only in between" (Buczynska-Garewicz 167). This statement refers to the philosophy of Jacques Derrida (b. 1930) who, in *Of Grammatology*, argues that meaning is never fully present in a word. An illusion of presence is created by the difference (*différence*) between the sounds of one word and those of another as well as by what Derrida calls *différance* or deferral. In other words, the formation of sense or meaning is constantly being postponed to the next sound or syllable as one reads. A suitable analogy may be the cinematic illusion of movement which is not a property of any single frame. In rejecting this line of thinking, Eco suggests that in Derrida's system, "language is caught in a play of multiple signifying games" because "a text cannot incorporate an absolute univocal meaning . . . which is continually deferred or delayed" (*The Limits* 33).

Between 1980 and 1995, Eco also wrote three novels: *The Name of the Rose* (1983), *Foucault's Pendulum* (1989), and *The Island of the Day Before* (1995). The novels are quite elaborate, indeed wondrous, illustrations of Eco's theories on semiotics and intertextuality (specifically, the quotes, allusions, and references relate one text to another), and they "drift" well beyond the boundaries or limits of the theoretical works mentioned above. In the present essay, however, I will focus on the representation of the writing and reading process in those novels—relating that process to Eco's statements of theory. Not only are they "possible worlds" and, therefore, reproduce through the process of representation aspects of specific cultures, sets of ideas or beliefs, and political systems, the novels indeed allude to or quote directly from dozens, if not hundreds, of historical documents and books from the periods in which the narratives are set: the Middle Ages, the modern period, and the seventeenth century, respectively. In the case of the last two novels, writers and readers are explicitly present in the texts. It is this transaction or negotiation of meaning conducted in the fictional works that I examine here.

In *The Name of the Rose*, the space of transaction of meaning and the tension between the two poles of closed and open interpretation is the library. It is housed within the imposing, indeed forbidding, walls of the Benedictine abbey where William of Baskerville and Adso of Melk are called upon to solve a series of gruesome murders. Said to contain the canonical works of Western civilization and guarded by a community of scholars who consider themselves to be "light to the whole known world, depository of knowledge, salvation of an ancient learning that threatened to disappear in fires, sacks, earthquakes" (henceforth *The Name* 36), the library is said to be, "[a] spiritual labyrinth, it is also a terrestrial labyrinth" (*The Name* 38). There are two types of books preserved here: sacred texts that are copied and read and pagan texts that are not read; the abbot tells the narrator (and the reader) that, "the monks . . . are in the scriptorium to carry out a precise task, which requires them to read certain volumes and not others, and not to pursue every foolish curiosity that seizes them" (*The Name* 37). In a way, neither set of texts is "open" to interpretation because the monks, and in particular the librarian, see themselves as "preserving, repeating, and defending the treasure of wisdom our fathers entrusted to them" (*The Name* 36). In addition, the labyrinthine structure of the library deprives them of the possibility of reading censored material. Only the librarian and assistant librarian have access to the code or key that permits entry into the inner sanctum where the forbidden books are, in a sense, imprisoned. The textual meaning is religiously believed to be antithetical to Christian dogma: "satanic verses" you might say. In a statement that is often repeated throughout the novel, the narrator points out that, "[t]he library was full of secrets, and especially of books that had never been given to the monks to read" (*The Name* 136).

Fanatical or dogmatic interpretation manifests itself in two ways in this novel: On the one hand, with respect to Scripture that is read univocally, i.e., it is interpreted with extreme single-mindedness, and on the other hand, one pre-Christian book in particular, is never read; it is, nevertheless, also interpreted fanatically or irrationally. In terms of the Scriptures, any aberrant or deviant interpretation is discouraged, indeed, punished as a heretical reading; it is even punishable by death. In fact, a great deal of the novel reproduces the fourteenth-century discourse on the Church's persecution of heretical orders. Additionally, rather than complement each other, different or contrasting versions of the biblical texts do not lead to synthesis but to discord. The narrator confirms this when he points out, "beyond this threshold . . . men have become one another's enemies through conflicting interpretations of the Bible" (*The Name* 330). In terms of the text not read, it is Aristotle's lost manuscript, the second book of the *Poetics*, allegedly dedicated to the topic of laughter. One key figure representing the attitude of fanatical fundamentalism (or censorship if you will) is the librarian, Jorge of Burgos, who is appropriately blind. He considers it as his personal responsibility to ensure the orthodox and unchallenged interpretation of the sacred texts, as well as to prevent the reading of the Aristotelian treatise, thought to be dangerous and capable of corrupting young, impressionable Christian minds. He is willing to go to any length, including murder and, eventually, the destruction of the entire library, in order to remain faithful to his reading of the Word of God and to the exclusion or suppression of "perverse literature." His views are conveyed aptly in this quote: "Jorge . . . said the psalms are the works of divine inspiration and use metaphors to convey the truth, while the works of the pagan poets use metaphors to convey falsehood" (*The Name* 111).

A second aspect of aberrant interpretation manifests itself when the first three of seven murders appear to be following a logical pattern. One of the "fanatical friars," Alinardo, reads the murders as acts performed in concert with the opening of the seven seals in the Apocalypse. Alinardo's remarks induce Baskerville, the detective, to speculate as follows: "The murderer did not strike at random, he was following a plan, . . . But is it possible to imagine a mind so evil that he kills only when he can do so while following the dictates of the book of the Apocalypse?" (*The Name* 364). This reading of the "signs" is so compelling that it induces our medieval Sherlock Holmes to think that it must be the correct interpretation, and it becomes his operative assumption as he proceeds with the investigation, that is until counterfacts oblige him to concede that this is an incorrect interpretation. There are several murderers with several quite different motives. The mania for seeing connections or relationships that seemed so logical turns out to be misguided or unguided. Each of the novels has a moment of epiphany or insight such as this, in which a carefully elaborated interpretative model collapses under the weight of its own premises. In this case, the detective is forced to admit: "There was no plot . . . and I discovered it by accident" (*The Name* 491).

In this novel, Eco is primarily concerned with exploring the textual mechanisms that encourage the reader to interpret the *fabula* or story in predictable ways as well suggesting methods for subverting the expectations of the reader in order to create an open work (critics are divided on whether *The Name of the Rose* is an "open" or "closed" narrative). The novel appears to demonstrate the insanity of an obsessively closed reading of texts—whether based on strict adherence to the literal sense of the words or on an equally rigid allegorical decipherment. It seems clear that in his first novel, as well as in *Foucault's Pendulum*, Eco is reproducing both the illustration and consequences of what may be called "esoteric knowledge" or knowledge intended for a privileged few and not meant for public dissemination. Even though in the Middle Ages pagan texts would have been read and studied by clerics, unlike the stark scenario constructed in the *Name of the Rose*, the frequency of the "forbidden text" theme, together with the conclusion of the novel strongly suggest that Eco's intention is to reject dogmatic or exclusive readings in favor of a public discourse or esoteric knowledge. The famous library, in the end, is burned to the ground: "The library had been doomed by its own impenetrability, by the mystery that protected it, by its few entrances" (*The Name* 489), observes the narrator, Adso. In addition, through the "rational" conjectures of the reader-detective Baskerville, the empirical or actual reader of *The Name of the Rose* comes to understand that, even if there is no final or definitive solution or ultimate interpretation (the transcendent signified of which semioticians speak), it is possible to identify distorted, indeed dangerous, ones. Franco Cardini speaks of the "dark fanaticism of the violent who are convinced that they have the truth in the palm of their hand and are prepared to do anything at all in order to impose it" (*Saggi* 27). They represent the practitioners of such an unacceptable interpretation.

For several critics, the novel can be interpreted as a dialogue or dialectic between an open and closed work: An opposition that, for some, is reducible to the intellectual (and eventually physical) confrontation between archenemies William of Baskervillle and Jorge of Burgos. The Englishman is a figure who stands for open inquiry of texts whereas the Spaniard stands for closure and an unreceptive stance with respect to approaches, in other words, readings other than his own. Walter Stephens suggests that, "[t]he duel between Jorge and William is . . . an allegory of the dialogue between the implied reader and the textual strategies through which the open text anticipates and provides its own predictions" (*Saggi* 145). The implied reader of whom Stephens is speaking is the reader whom the text assumes. In presenting the closed-minded monks by the blind librarian, who is so opposed to laughter, challenged by the model detective Baskerville (or perfect reader anticipated by Eco), and who is eventually overtaken by the narrative he is struggling to solve, Eco appears to be offering the possibility of endless interpretation. However, some period of time after the publication of *The Name of the Rose*, he qualifies such a response to his text on the part of some critics as "overinterpretation"—which is to say, he accuses those critics of finding associations, connections, and meanings the text does not actually advocate.

The two later novels present a considerably more complex structure. They correspond to the evolving views of Umberto Eco on the reading dynamic as well as his efforts to identify those "boundaries" that guide interpretation. In *Foucault's Pendulum*, we not only have the same dizzying frequency of references to volumes written from medieval to modern times, but we actually have an author/writer and a reader embedded in the text. Books are cited in the context of research on the history of the Templars and other secret societies from the time of the Crusades to the present, carried out by Casaubon, Belbo, and Diotallevi (the principal characters in the story) for the purpose of producing a publication, *Isis Unveiled*, for the Milanese Garamond Press, in 1968. Their bibliographical investigations lead them to countless books on the Templars, the Society of the Rosy Cross, and the Cabalists. Eventually, they uncover connections among many of the books, with the basic assumption being that these various societies conspired through the centuries to conceal some enormous secret. One character speculates: "Suppose the Templars had a plan to conquer the world and they knew the secret of an immense source of power" (henceforth *Pendulum* 90). The catalyst for the investigation and interpretation of the existence of a plan of this type is the discovery of a cryptic fragment of writing, a sort of Rosetta stone, which the three detectives painstakingly decode. Casaubon muses:

> Suddenly it all seemed to come together: satanic and Moorish rites in the Temple of Jerusalem, African witchcraft for the sub-proletarians of the Brazilian Northeast, the message of Provins with its hundred and twenty years, and the hundred and twenty years of the Rosicrucians. (*Pendulum* 146)

The readers in the novel, then, are not only Casaubon, Belbo, and Diotallevi, but all the readers of the past who fanatically saw or imagined connections among social, political, scientific, and natural events throughout the ages and transformed legend and myth into virtual reality. They are represented by contemporary characters such as a Colonel Ardenti and Agliè, both of whom have an unusually intense interest in the findings of the novel's protagonists. In their undeterred intention to uncover associations and links, even where there is no logical reason to suppose these exist, the characters are designed or "intended" to demonstrate what Eco likes to call "overinterpretation" or "adventurous misreading." In one of his theoretical works he tells us as much when he suggests that it is "the same technique implemented by contemporary readers who wander through texts in order to find in them secret puns, unheard-of etymologies, unconscious links, chances of 'Slipping Beauties'" (*The Limits* 26).

In order to demonstrate further, and simultaneously undercut, the "unlimited semiosis" contrived to conceal a "secret message" (the alleged cosmic plot or metaconspiracy theory, which is a theory about conspiracy theories), Eco has his protagonists invent the idea of writing a book themselves. In this book they, in fact, claim to have solved the centuries-old riddle, which is the location of the core or control point of the telluric currents or the earth's electromagnetic field. The pendulum (hence the title of the book) is supposed to be the key to the secret, for, at exactly midnight on a given date, it is to point to a predetermined item on a map and thereby reveal the truth: "We . . . insisted on playing games with the Diabolicals, on showing them that if there had to be a cosmic plot, we could invent the most cosmic of all" (*Pendulum* 364), reflects the narrator Casaubon.

The "first author" is Jacopo Belbo and his writing tool is a computer named Abulafia. Eco demonstrates the procedure of "Hermetic semiosis" not only through the connections, both real and imagined, established among the most unrelated occurrences on the part of the so-called Diabolicals, but he also does so through Belbo's approach to the creation of his "novel." The character feeds random fragments of information borrowed from the hundreds of sources—both historical and fictional—into the database, along with some syntactical connectors. Then he programs the computer to generate a continuous narrative, which ends up sounding remarkably legible and compelling. So much so, in fact, that the suspicious and persistent Diabolicals eventually break into Belbo's computer and are so completely convinced of the correctness of their interpretation of the fabulous *fabula* (or tale) that they eventually arrange to have Belbo killed in order to prevent his secret from being divulged or interpreted (the author is dead in more ways than one in Eco's fictional world). The critique of uncontrolled free association is best conveyed with the last words of coauthor Diotallevi who says: "I'm dying because I convinced myself that there was no order, that you could do whatever you liked with any text. I spent myself convincing myself of this" (*Pendulum* 468).

The epiphany occurs when Lorenza utilizes her interpretative competence to "correct" the (mis)reading of the fourteenth-century Provins parchment—she demonstrates that, instead of a vitally important hermetic code to be painstakingly broken, it is nothing more than a laundry list. This "apocalyptic" moment recalls the instance in *The Name of the Rose* in which detective Baskerville comes to the realization that his logical assumptions about the series of murders, i.e., his interpretative procedures, are rendered invalid by evidence of an alternative explanation or interpretation of the facts. If it illustrates the obsession with finding or establishing relationships among unrelated objects and events, simply to make one's dogmatic interpretation coherent, *Foucault's Pendulum* also puts on display some of the strategies that can counteract that obsession. One of these is the careful, indeed meticulous philological reconstruction of relevant texts by Casaubon and his associates. This reconstruction exposes flaws, errors, miscalculations, and lacunae in the readings of the same texts by the Diabolicals who are this novel's counterparts to the fanatical Benedictines of *The Name of the Rose*. Another is, as stated, the disclosure of Lorenza who subjects the temporarily correct reading of Casaubon and his associates to her own scrutiny. Through this narrative twist, Eco appears to exhibit his faith in the power of reason, if not to achieve absolute truths, at least to unmask illusions of truth. In one of his theoretical works, Eco writes: "It is possible to reach an agreement, if not about the meanings that a text encourages, at least about those that a text discourages" (*The Limits* 42).

In his 1995 novel, *The Island of the Day Before*, which also contains an author (as well as a narrator), who also happens to be the reader of his own fiction, Eco searches for the parameters of legitimate interpretation, his personal "Foucault's pendulum" as it were. Eco operates on four premises:

1. On the basis of his own theorization of concepts, such as the model reader, specifically, the ideal reader envisioned by the author, one who is capable of catching all the clues and cashing in all the metaphors, allusions, and connotations dispensed by the author;
2. the interdependence of the *intentio auctoris*, the *intentio operis*, and the *intentio lectoris*, i.e., the intention of the author, of the text, and of the reader;
3. encyclopedic competence, or the ability to cross reference;

4. contextual logic, rational conjecture, and universes of discourse, i.e., the diction or subject matter of specific discipline.

By using these four concepts, Eco constructs a novel within a novel, both to illustrate these interpretive strategies or prerequisites as well as to suggest plausible remedies, if not precise rules, for the avoidance or containment of "Hermetic drift." This concept, as we have seen, is the tendency to make arbitrary and unsupported connections. Some critics are not necessarily convinced that Eco succeeds completely in resolving the thorny issue of the "role of the reader" and accuse him of indulging in the very practice he wants to discourage, if not erase. Bouchard, for instance, expresses the following reservations about Eco's procedure:

> This [*The Island of the Day Before*] is also a contradictory, ambivalent text; a novel which voices Eco's latest theoretical stance against aberrant, Hermetic models of semiotic creativity, while coming perhaps dangerously close to reproducing precisely a definitional expenditure, that "excess of wonder" that he had set out to critique. (*Reading Eco* 351)

The protagonist is Roberto de la Griva, shipwrecked in the South Pacific in 1643. He has been sent by Cardinal Richelieu to spy on Admiral Byrd, who is on a secret mission to solve the problem of the measurement of longitude. Byrd's ship, the *Amaryllis*, has been destroyed in a storm, and Roberto has survived by floating on a plank until he lands on an abandoned ship called the *Daphne*. As it turns out, our "Robinson Eco" cannot swim and is stranded on a deserted ship, anchored near an unreachable island. He soon learns that, separating him from that island, there is the 180th meridian, the International Date Line *ante litteram*; hence, the island is located in the past relative to the observer. In order to keep himself from going insane, he writes letters to a woman, in which he describes his experiences. The storyteller claims to have found those letters and has interpreted their content in the creation of his novel, that is, *The Island of the Day Before*. Although much of the novel provides a virtual workshop on the process of unlimited semiosis, the aspects of the text that best represent this activity are the quest for the *punto fijo* or fixed point and the meanings associated with the "orange dove." In terms of the elusive "fixed point" from which lines of longitude could be measured, many historical figures are driven in their quest for this "holy grail" or "Foucault's pendulum." Figures such as Colbert, Mazarin, and Byrd's crew search on the basis of the application of salves. Bouchard tells us: "Since such experiments derive from the theoretical premise of universal sympathy and analogy, they are but the 'empirical' side of Hermetic semiosis" (*Reading Eco* 356). This group of *personae* can be equated with the fanatical "raiders of the lost Temple," as well as with the secretive community of Benedictine scholars of the narratives cited previously.

In addition to focusing on the conduct of the figures mentioned above, Eco's narrator also illustrates the notion of unlimited association or the mania for seeing connections by devoting eight full pages to the innumerable meanings that have been attributed to the dove across the ages. He is inclined to entitle this digression, "Explication of the Dove." Tracing the semantic value of the term from the Egyptians to his day, the narrator offers the following conclusion: "The reader may think that the dove has all too many meanings. But if a symbol or hieroglyph must be chosen as something to die for, its meaning should be multiple" (henceforth *The Island* 352). It appears that Eco's narrator indulges in this lengthy exercise in semantics and etymology to present in his narrative the eighteenth-century obsession with the search for secret meanings (i.e., hermetic semiosis) by establishing relationships among disparate objects on the basis of appearance, linguistic similarity, behavior, and so forth. However, the same procedure also demonstrates one of the primary requirements of the model reader theorized by Eco, namely, "encyclopedic knowledge." In other words, in order to recover all of the allusions (intertexts) hidden beneath the surface of the text by the author, the reader must have the capacity to uncover all possible associations by calling upon his or her knowledge of the items named in the discourse from every conceivable point of view. In commenting on the work of Eco, one Italian critic makes this point precisely: "The encyclopedia is dominated, however, by the principle of interpretation, of unlimited semiosis" (Cantarano 234, my translation).

In addition to the letters that form the bulk of *The Island of the Day Before*, Roberto writes a novel of his own. The principal actors in his story are: he, Lilia, a lady he met in Paris some time prior to his misadventure on the high seas and to whom he has written but not sent love letters, an imaginary evil twin brother named Ferrante, and the elusive island. The narrator of *The Island of the Day Before* informs the reader that Roberto's novel is a typical romance in content and structure, containing as it does equal proportions of intrigue, adventure, and love. That same narrator functions as the model reader of Roberto's narrative in that he interprets the tale, fills in gaps, conjectures along with the protagonist, and anticipates elements of the plot (or diegesis).

Where does aberrant interpretation or "hermetic drift" come in? It is quite evident that Eco is talking about this narrative phenomenon because *The Island of the Day Before* concludes with Roberto floating on a board, toward the island, he thinks. However, the currents cause him to drift into infinity along the imaginary line that divides past and present. Another character, Father Caspar, a Leonardo Da Vinci and Galileo amalgam, had disappeared beneath the same waters in his anachronistic submarine, in a desperate attempt to go ashore himself. As in *Foucault's Pendulum*, we are once again confronted with the death of the author, murdered by his own fiction, in a sense, and by an excess of interpretation on the part of the reader. This excess in Roberto's tale assumes the form of some implausible connections made by the character/narrator (Roberto), who is also an interpreter of historical events, of his own present circumstances, and of the fictional elements of the romances he has read in the past. Eventually, all of these "agents of the imagination" blur the line that separates not only Roberto from the island but also reality from fiction: "Roberto . . . had finally come to make the two universes [the real and the fictional] flow effortlessly one into the other, and he mingled their laws" (*The Island* 497). He is guilty of overinterpreting his own narrative and must pay the price, so to speak.

How does he reach this point? The answer lies in the reason that Roberto sets out on his fatal journey to an island he is destined never to reach. His motivation for undertaking the risky voyage into the unknown is that, confusing the narrated and the real, he has placed his evil brother Ferrante on the island to which his Lady Lilia is now floating on a raft—having been set adrift on the ocean in Roberto's tale, that is. In order to intercept his fictionalized Lady and prevent her fictional abduction by his imaginary rival, Roberto "takes the plunge." The narrator speculates as follows on this action: "Is it possible he [Roberto] did not realize that he was planning to land in reality on the Island to rescue a woman who was arriving there only through his narrative?" (*The Island* 497).

The conclusion of *The Island of the Day Before* appears to be an apt synthesis of some important aspects of Umberto Eco's theoretical work. By having his protagonist novelist drift into the sunset riding the dividing line between today and yesterday, Eco appears to be giving metaphorical expression to his personal quest for balance between the extremes of textual enslavement and interpretive anarchy. More specifically, he distinguishes between absolute loyalty to the "letter of the text" and the intentions of the author who shaped the text on the one hand and absolute freedom to read the text in any idiosyncratic or subjective way possible on the other. The boundaries, as defined in the novels and in the theoretical works listed at the top of this essay, are embedded partly in the novel and partly in the linguistic, cultural, literary competence of the Model Reader projected by and in the text. To extend Eco's metaphor, it would appear that "appropriate" reading is navigating the sea of textuality while avoiding both the Scylla of dogmatism and the Charybdis of hermeneutic dispersal.

Works Cited

Bouchard, Norma. "Whose 'Excess of Wonder' Is It Anyway? Reading Umberto Eco's Tangle of Hermetic and Pragmatic Semiosis in *The Island of the Day Before*." *Reading Eco: An Anthology*. Ed. Rocco Capozzi. Bloomington: Indiana University Press, 1997. 350–61.

Buczynska-Garewicz, Hanna. "Semiotics and Deconstruction." Capozzi, *Reading Eco*, 163–72.

Cantarano, Giuseppe. *Immagini del nulla*. Milano: Mondadori, 1998.

Capozzi, Rocco. "Umberto Eco." *Encyclopedia of Contemporary Literary Theory: Approaches, Scholars, Terms*. Ed. Irena R. Makaryk. Toronto: University of Toronto Press, 1993. 303.

Cardini, Franco. "Clericus in labyrintho." *Saggi su Il nome della rosa*. Ed. Renato Giovannoli. Milan: Bompiani, 1985. 21–32.

Derrida, Jacques. *Of Grammatology*. Trans. Gayatri C. Spivak. Baltimore: Johns Hopkins University Press, 1976.

Eco, Umberto. *Foucault's Pendulum*. Trans. William Weaver. New York: Ballantine Books, 1989.

———. *Interpretation and Overinterpretation*. Ed. Stefan Collini. Cambridge: Cambridge University Press, 1992.

———. *The Island of the Day Before*. Trans. William Weaver. New York: Penguin Books, 1995.

———. *The Limits of Interpretation*. Bloomington: Indiana University Press, 1990.

———. *Misreadings*. Trans. William Weaver. London: Jonathan Cape, 1993.

———. *The Name of the Rose*. Trans. William Weaver. San Diego: Harcourt Brace Jovanovich, 1983.

———. *The Role of the Reader. Explorations in the Semiotics of Texts*. Bloomington: Indiana University Press, 1979.

———. *Semiotics and the Philosophy of Language*. London: MacMillan, 1984.

———. *Six Walks in the Fictional Woods*. Cambridge: Harvard University Press, 1994.

———. *A Theory of Semiotics*. Bloomington: Indiana University Press, 1976.

———. *Opera aperta*. Milan: Bompiani, 1962 (Selections translated as *The Open Work* by Anna Cancogni. Cambridge: Harvard University Press, 1989).

Francese, Joseph. *Narrating Postmodern Time and Space*. Albany: State University of New York Press, 1997.

Stephens, Walter E. "Un Eco in fabula." Cardini, *Saggi su Il nome della rosa*, 127–53.

Tejera, Victorino. "Eco, Peirce, and the Necessity of Interpretation." Capozzi, *Reading Eco,* 147–62.

4

Voices of Conscience: The Power of Language in the Latin American *Testimonio*

Elena De Costa

One of the major contributions to literary studies in recent years has been the recognition that sociopolitical consciousness is invariably fused with aesthetic practice. Contemporary Latin American literature abounds with documentary or nonfiction narratives based on historically documented and/or personally experienced (but unrecorded) events, which are given an explicit narrative framework by an intervening narrator. Such works are routinely characterized as predominantly social testimonials. Testimonies are typically personal accounts that usually assume one of the three narrative structures. They are written in the first or third person or have the form of an interview. Testimonial writing reflects through language present circumstance as it engages the reader in its unraveling of a people's situation and its appeal for changes. However, at a sociocultural level, testimonial narratives are in stark contrast to the traditions of many indigenous societies where traditional oral culture is pitted against literary Western culture based on an abstract form of communication: writing. Thus, the testimonial narrative becomes a battleground of sorts between these two manifestations of language, where traditional cultural norms are placed in direct conflict with the modern hegemonic device of writing. To some extent, in many testimonial texts the spoken word may acquire power as an instrument of action and dominance over described reality. Furthermore, psychodynamic elements of orality—proverbs, sayings, popular verses, and songs, even onomatopoeic sounds—often form part of the linguistic scaffolding of these orally produced texts. Nevertheless, regardless of the implications of orality versus the written text, literary testimony contributes not only to the revitalization of realism but to the reconstruction of the social subject as testimonial narratives retrieve the historical memory of a people. It is the function of the testimonial narrative, despite its first-person narrative perspective, to look into the people's social consciousness by bringing history into literature and literary mechanism back into reality. Historical laws and social movements can be appreciated in the characters, whereas ideological statements are voiced through the author-narrator, who is often a real protagonist or witness of the events he or she recounts and whose unit of narration is usually a "life" or a significant life experience. For the reader, the implications of the opposition of orality to written language are understood and appreciated on the level of polemical metacommentary. The text becomes a collective voice, representing the anonymous voice and consciousness of the people.

Latin American testimonial narrative or "literature" of witness establishes a symbiotic relationship between producer of the text (author) and the narrator or historical witness. Furthermore, this hybrid form of literary expression carves its space out of documentary writing, autobiographical report, eyewitness literature, the literature of resistance and protest, and the New Testament. The embrace of the "apocalypse now" paradoxically separates the *testimonio* from its closest forerunners: the nonfiction novel, new journalism, the ethnic cultural narratives, and the social or anthropological documents on the "culture of poverty" popularized by Oscar Lewis in *The Children of Sánchez*. Toward the end of the 1970s, in contrast to earlier testimonials in the region, these narratives no longer focused on the heroes of important historical events but on the everyday person. It is within this testimonial tradition, whose intention is the vindication of the marginalized voices devoid of a historical context, that the works of this most recent and controversial narrative form must be placed. The testimonial genre is positioned at the margins, where it offers a voice for the voiceless, that is, peasants, indigenous peoples, women, children, homosexuals, the poor, political prisoners, guerrilla fighters, and others who have been discredited, disenfranchised, or dispossessed. The testimonial function, in its inevitable incorporation of oral history and popular idiom within the context of its heterogeneity, multiplicity of voices decentering of the authorial figure, and its tendency toward fragmentation, is, in effect, an attempt to redefine art. The final product is a hybrid of conversation and writing, of reporting and recreating, thus reflecting within its very form the issues of memory, recording, and storytelling that are at the core of the testimonial narrative.[1]

Although testimony is not a new genre, since it derives from a long oral history of witnessing of various forms, what is of literary interest is the collective narrative structure of such works. The collective narration is given the framework of a single voice, which narrates lived experiences representative of the cultural as well as the personal circumstance. The goal of the narrative voice becomes the act of revelation for the reader in the act of recreation of personal experiences, witnessed events, cultural perceptions, traditional values, and a newly acquired sociopolitical consciousness. The narrator's discourse, even while exploring past remembrances of childhood or adulthood, in effect, becomes a collective narrative. The culture and community of origin represented in the narrative voice enable the text's I-discourse to be considered as part of a community building we-discourse of communal fate. Thus, the testimonial "I" in Rigoberta Menchú's narration, *I, Rigoberta Menchú, An Indian Woman in Guatemala* (*Me llamo Rigoberta Menchú y así me nació la conciencia*) assembles her community (the Quiché-speaking Indians of the Western Highlands of Guatemala) by extension, taking great pains not to substitute her communal voice in a totalizing gesture. Instead, it would seem that the implied and often explicitly "plural subject" of testimony needs the singularity of first-person autobiographical narrative in this text. This testimonial "I" invites the reader to be with the speaker and among her people. Rather than identifying with the narrative voice or its collective whole, as is the case of the traditional autobiographical text, the reader becomes a participant. Thus, unlike the private and even lonely moment of autobiographical writing (often producing a personal and distinctive style as part of the individuation process), the testimonial account becomes a public event in which the collective self strives to preserve an interpersonal rhetoric (a reflection of its oral-based origins), which invites the complicity of the reader. Once the subject of the testimonial is understood as the community made up of a variety of roles, the reader is called upon to become a participatory voice, an accomplice (but not an intimate member) of the community of testimonial voices, a constellation of discourses, which testify to unspeakable acts in the text.

The problematics of this most recent literary genre start with the selection and presentation of the protagonists, oftentimes political activists or labor union leaders who are presented as quite ordinary individuals, the "self-representation" of the Other. The subtitles and translations tend to stress this aspect of the commoner: *An Indian Woman in Guatemala*, *A Woman of the Bolivian Mines*, *A Peruvian Peasant Speaks*, *A Runaway Slave*. One of the most haunting questions plaguing the *testimonio,* and indeed all forms of witness-bearing accounts, is whether the testimony of a witness trying to recall an event or series of events quite removed from the present time could be considered credible. If memory is not only subjugated to the distortions of time but also corrupted by the perceptions the present imposes upon a traumatic past, in what way, if any, is the contemporary testimonial narrative accurate in its portrayal of events? Although the preselected witnesses appear to speak in the first person, who is actually in control of their words? Who, in fact, is the authorial voice? The legal liability of the situation is exposed in translations which upgrade the characters to "authors" and reclassify the authors of the Spanish texts as "editors" or "transcribers" of oral transmissions or even "collaborators," or "coauthors." The author of the biography of a runaway slave in Miguel Barnet's text, for example, becomes the editor of an autobiography supposedly authored by the illiterate Esteban Montejo, the work's protagonist. The point here is not so much that characters and authors appear to be reversible legal and literary fictions but rather that these witnesses take control of their authentic voice and use language to create a real, immediate, relivable environment of memorable events. The use of a mode of thought dominated by orality (parallelisms, antitheses, epithets, moral sayings, prayers, legends, and other such forms of social interaction in the community) demonstrates collective moral values, approved behavior codes of the community represented by the testimonial witness. Orality thus becomes a mechanism to depersonalize on one level the testimonial voice and create a collective vision as public act on another. Indeed, such texts attribute their unique problematic texture to the inevitable tensions between the process of remembering events as situational moments and writing history as an elaboration of events in an analytical, systematized, more abstract format.

Beyond these obvious problems, there are additional concerns related to the Latin American *testimonio* which might cause further reflection on the historical nature of the *relato* or storytelling account. These include the memory and the self-censorship of the interviewee, the invasiveness of the interview technique, in spite of the proclaimed self-effacement of the interviewer, and the editing process, producing a narrative from a log of interviews and dialogues. The transposition of the dialogic process (orality) into the literary form of the written word focusing on a selected sequence of events (an overarching theme) and a message with sociopolitical implications only imposes an additional layer of textual complexity that mediates between the authentic word and world of the reader/spectator, who often is enlisted as a collaborative participant in a continuation (toward possible resolution) of real-life events outside of the text. Thus, the testimonial narrative expresses the urgency of victims whose eyewitness accounts seek redress and justice and challenge official discourse.[2]

Bearing Witness: Testimony and Survival

Although the testimonial narrative has been recently accepted into the literary canon, placed in its proper context, testimonial storytelling is not really a new genre. It derives from a long oral history of witnessing. The doubling of this oral history into a public plea merely marks the coalescence of a number of historical developments in economics, in literature, and in politics in Latin America. Testimony is the narrative's address to hearing. Perhaps a key feature of the *testimonio* is not that its marginalized voices are suddenly speaking for themselves but rather those of us outside the network are finally hearing them for the first time. In this sense then, the task of the interviewer (collaborator, authorial voice, co-author, editor) is to be unobtrusively present throughout the testimonial account in order to keep alive the witnessing narration. The testimonial process is a dialogue with a willing listener wherein, apart from socio-political realities, the witness to the trauma, the listener of the tale and the ultimate reader/recipient are made to confront existential questions that tend to be displaced from day-to-day living. These are the all-encompassing, vexing issues that raise the testimonial narrative from the level of a call to political activism or propaganda to the realm of literature—the question of facing death; of facing time and its passage; of the meaning and purpose of living; of the limits of one's potential; of losing the ones who are close to us; the great question of our ultimate aloneness; our otherness from any other; our responsibility to and for our destiny; the question of forgiveness and its limits. On this basis, the testimonial genre has been allowed inclusion into an enlarged, multicultural literary canon.[3] In the wake of the atrocities documented in Latin America in recent decades, the testimonial narrative with its authorial presence, its collective voice, its sometimes inaccurate account of details does authentically recreate the prevailing texture of a region during a particular frame of time. Undeniably, in many of the military regimes throughout Latin America in the twentieth century, cultural values, political conventions, social mores, national identities, families, and institutions lost their context. Repossessing one's life story through giving testimony is itself a form of action, of change necessary to complete the process of survival after traumatic events have been experienced.[4]

Remembered Lives: Collaborative Storytelling—A Measure of Memory and Identity

This discourse leads us to the question of the guiding narrational voice, the so-called "absent voice" in the testimonial, whose function is to guide the comprehension of events through its presentation of incidents, providing a kind of coherence through its textual mediations. It must be recalled, however, that the narrative voice in testimonial literature is a collective enterprise: The protagonist testifies as an autobiographical voice (a signatory first-person narration), representative of the experiences of a larger group unwilling or unable to find a public discourse. It is the interviewer (as solicitor and receiver of the testimonies) who provides a vehicle (the literary text) that presents the realities of the testimonial voice to a larger Western audience. Hence, the testimony is organized in such a way that it is raised to the level of inquiry of universal significance. The narrative voice becomes the subject of a quest concerning what the experiences testify to; the witness becomes a questioner, and the asker is perceived as not merely a factual investigator but as the bearer of the testimonial's philosophical address and inquiry. In short, the *testimonio*'s *other* voice is neither the last word of knowledge nor the ultimate authority on the historical events narrated, but one more topographical and cognitive position of yet another witness—the reader. Rigoberta Menchú, Esteban Montejo, and Jesusa Palancares (Josefina Bórquez) collaborate to ensure that the social questions raised in their texts will continue to be pondered by the reader. The inquirer, in other words, not merely raises these questions of enduring historical importance but is also the source that takes apart all previous answers of the oftentimes one-sided distorted official story of authoritarian regimes by offering an alternative version of a broken silence.

In recent decades reader response criticism has focused on the role of the reader.[5] The reader is no longer a passive receiver of the meaning inherent in the narrative text but an active participant in the actualization—indeed, the production—of textual meaning as an interpretive accomplishment, much like members of an oral storytelling audience.[6] One also finds in reader response criticism and other lines of analysis convergent with it a concern with the formal devices authors employ to engage the participatory involvement of the reader.[7] These devices are the textual creation of a communicative context for the narration, the leaving of gaps to be filled by the reader, and so on. The effort to resituate the literary narrative text in general, and the testimonial narrative in particular, in a web of communicative relationships and processes has induced some literary theorists to begin to consider literary narration as akin to storytelling.[8] Narrative in the *testimonio* becomes in this context not merely the reflection of culture but indeed the constituent of social life in the act of storytelling. Beneath the story line there is a deep sense of social action, which is essential to the conception of the testimonial narrative as social practice (not merely literary exposure and denunciation).

Guatemala's Rigoberta Menchú, and Venezuela's Anthropologist Elisabeth Burgos-Debray: A Collective Voice

Guatemala's Nobel Prize laureate, Rigoberta Menchú, is a case in point. For as much as the narrating voice reveals herself, her indigenous heritage, and indigenous peoples' contemporary status in Guatemalan society, *I, Rigoberta Menchú, an Indian Woman in Guatemala* also turns the inward-looking discourse outward toward the reader. This pseudo-autobiography becomes both dialogic encounter and personal self-reflection on social issues raised in her witnessing account. In this regard, the testimonial narrative transcribed from oral discourse clearly demonstrates its linkage to the autobiographical genre. Autobiography clearly is protean in character, encompassing a multiplicity of literary forms, testimonial discourse among them. One critic, James Olney, suggests this process of reader self-discovery while reflecting on autobiographical writings,

> Autobiography . . . offer[s] us understanding that is finally not of someone else but of ourselves. . . . As readers we go to history, as to philosophy, to autobiography and poetry, to learn more not about other people but about ourselves and the present . . . What one seeks in reading autobiography is not a date, a name, or a place, but a characteristic way of perceiving, of organizing, and of understanding, an individual way of feeling and expressing that one can somehow relate to oneself ... and, like the poet, the autobiographer who draws out of the flux of events a coherent pattern, or who creates a sufficient metaphor for experience, discovers in the particular, and reveals to us, the universal.[9]

Such awareness of self naturally occurs while we listen to the words of a dramatic character on stage or read statements made by fictional or nonfictional figures rather than by a detached, omniscient narrator. Seemingly authorial sentences such as "This is, in part, recalling history and, in part, a call to awareness" (Olney 67); "We began to understand that the root of all our problems was exploitation" (Olney 118); and "And I began to discover many things that I hadn't experienced but that many others had" (Olney 165).[10] Such comments cause a similar identification with the collective consciousness perspective in the work. This is so only because such statements strike us as having greater validity if we assume that a mind (or minds) other than the narrator's (or testimonial voice's) is responsible for their meaning. Since Rigoberta Menchú employs both direct and indirect forms of discourse with a verbalization of collective beliefs (often using the first-person plural as representative of the regional indigenous populace) throughout her testimonial text, in such cases she is substituting her words for an individual's speech, thought, or sensory perception. This type of literary discourse is substitutionary narration.[11] Rather than detract from the dominant first-person singular narration, the substitutionary narrative throws the inner voice of the testimonial voice of self and other in high relief. In this dual discourse the narrating voice and the voices of her people (as individuals and as a collective) speak simultaneously or, more precisely, the narrator says *in propria persona* what her nonfictional characters mean. When Rigoberta speaks, she does so on behalf of the whole collective, using the first-person singular precisely because she has been authorized to speak out of the one mind of consensus, accountable to the collective for her words. The testimonial voice, Rigoberta Menchú, not only speaks the words "Everything in our lives is like a film. Constant suffering" (116), but experiences them as they emerge from her consciousness and the consciousness of those who populate her narration. This element of experienced speech renders greater universal appeal to the text and expands its focus from the life of a single individual to that of an entire people, an ethnography composed through an autobiographical perspective. The personal and social obligations the testimonial account imposes on the narrator broaden its scope to the point that the text, at times, seems to pay homage more to its voiceless characters given a voice through the author than to the authorial voice herself. For example, Rigoberta makes the following observation: "We have to keep this grief as a testimony to them because they never exposed their lives even when their grief was great too" (199). Rather than being a retrospective account of a single life, Rigoberta Menchú's text becomes an autobiographical testimonial to the lives of a people both living and dead, ancestors from the distant past and future generations yet to be born. In this wider context of a ritualized past, an oppressive present, and a future based on sacred prophecies, the text can be viewed as much more than the life of an individual, family, or localized population. The passages from the sacred books of the *Popul vuh, Chilam Balam,* and the Bible opening each chapter together with the cultural information both revealed and withheld in this continuous monologue-like narrative, act as framing devices for the text's resonance of confident memory. Indeed, it is a sanctified memory that extends beyond that of private and public lives. Ritual-generated experience and ritual-generated knowledge open zones of thought and feeling at once collective, cumulative, and transformative. In a similar vein, the recollection of sacred texts and cultural secrets of long-evolved strategies for survival surpass immediate emotional experiences, leading to deeper understandings (". . . all this gave me a lot to think about" (208). " . . . I am open to life" (224).

Mexico's Elena Poniatowska and Josefina Bórquez: A Dual Voice

The renowned Mexican novelist Elena Poniatowska, unlike the mediating voice in Rigoberta Menchú's account, not only interviews her subject from a writer's standpoint but also gets to know her at a human level over a lengthy period in her testimonial text *Until We Meet Again*. The underprivileged Jesusa Palancares (a fictionalization of a poor Mexican woman named Josefina Bórquez, interviewed and befriended by the author over a number of years) entertains the reader with her narrative style imbued with an oral quality and packed with anecdotes of a life full of unconventional adventure. Jesusa takes her listener through a journey of stories, the key events and experiences of her life: her early memories of her mother's death and her childhood with her father and her brothers and sister; her troubled relationships with a series of stepmothers; her adventures while following her father, and later her violent husband in the Mexican Revolution; her experiences in Mexico City in a variety of jobs and often makeshift homes; and her involvement with the Spiritist Church. She provides a full commentary on all these experiences, revealing belief systems stemming from popular wisdom, popular prejudices, and church dogma. The result is a rich, often contradictory, and always interesting word stream—a series of interwoven tales of a life lived to the fullest (the real Jesusa lived from 1900–1987), often under duress due to her impoverished situation. The hardships faced by this testimonial figure and many of the circumstances in which she finds herself serve to convert the text into a valuable social document. These aspects provide the testimonial elements of the text. Relying on experience, Jesusa bears witness and exposes the failings of revolutionary and post-revolutionary Mexico. The reader learns about the poor conditions of employment for illiterate women with no alternative income, the abuses committed by middle-and upper-class women against their servants, the violence committed by men against women, and the complete lack of any state support for all, even for those who, like Jesusa, are widows of fighters in the Revolution. The power of language to reproduce visually these still-life portraits (Jesusa does not come across as symbol, metaphor, or archetype) engage us by their simplicity as she assesses her own place in her society, instantly negating years of state rhetoric: "When all's said and done I've got no country . . . I don't feel Mexican and I don't recognize the Mexicans. Here, there's nothing more than greed and self-interest. If I had money and possessions I'd be Mexican, but as I'm worse than garbage, I'm nothing at all . . . " (*Until We Meet Again* 232).

Poniatowska readily makes the distinction between the testimonial as a literary piece and anthropological and sociological accounts when she states ". . . my work may be viewed as a testimonial novel and not an anthropological or sociological document. I made use of the anecdotes, the ideas and many of Jesusa Palancares' expressions, but I would never be able to assert that the narrative is a direct transcription of her life because she herself would reject that" ("And Here's to You Jesusa" 151).

In order to avoid the erasure of Third-World misery—the misery of solitude, displacement, and indifference—Poniatowska allies herself with the oppressed and allows her characters to voice their thoughts in her works. No longer the literature of confessions, diaries, intimist descriptions, these pseudo-autobiographical Latin American narratives become, in effect, politically committed literature. The very purpose of this literary form is explained by Elena Poniatowska herself. Referring to the Latin American contemporary writer, she says

> We write in order to understand the incomprehensible, in order to bear testimony of things, so that our children's children will know. We write in order to be. We write so as not to be wiped off from the map. In Latin America, we write because this is the only way we know not to disappear, and in order to bear testimony about those who disappear because of politics or hunger. ("Women and Literature" 86–87)

Cuba's Miguel Barnet

The founder of the testimonial genre contributes most to the confusion of this literary form as biography or autobiography.[12] Miguel Barnet's *relato de vida,* in very much the same vein as Poniatowska's work, carries to its ultimate consequences both the act of transmission of the memories of another and the appropriation of those memories by the recipient of that transmission. In this testimonial narrative, Cuban novelist and anthropologist Miguel Barnet presents the narrative of 105-year-old

Esteban Montejo, who lived as a slave, as fugitive in the wilderness, and as a soldier in the Cuban war of independence. Honest, blunt, compassionate, shrewd, and engaging, his voice provides an extraordinary insight into the African culture that took root in the Caribbean. The text's contribution to our understanding of Cuban history and national temperament is no less than its immense appeal as a human testament. All the fire and dash of the Cuban character, the refusal ever to cringe or to surrender to misfortune, take on flesh and meaning in the reminiscences of this stubborn veteran invested with historical significance. In his body of literary production, Barnet uses a direct, frank discourse, always colloquial, sometimes furnished with metaphor, but directed at real things within an imaginative and colorful world. Barnet has attributed his prosaic style to the influence of the Cuban Revolution, with its plain, direct language used both for speeches and in everyday language. Barnet has spoken at length about the relationship testimonial narrative establishes between the producer of the text (author) and the narrator or historical witness, who is presented to the reader as the real author. The symbiosis once again reflects the ambivalence between reality and fiction, or more specifically in the testimonial novel, between historical memory and fiction. The ostensible mission of this narrative, as is the case with the texts that have continued its tradition, was to record living history and, more specifically, to challenge "official," bourgeois history, to fill the voids in the record and thus to empower the voice of the underprivileged and the repressed. For the most part, this witness-voice has been a representative of the ongoing social struggles from the revolutionary (sometimes directly Marxist) point of view. In *testimonio* the "other" who is called to action is meant to be "us," enlisted collaborators in the struggle for social justice. The foundational value of *The Autobiography of a Runaway Slave* lies in Barnet's recovery of a specific Cuban and Caribbean cultural history, and the biography of the former slave is actually left incomplete at the beginning of this century. The emphasis on cultural anthropology, which turns the narrative into an encyclopedia of cultural history, characterizes some other better-known testimonial works discussed herein, such as Poniatowska's *Until We Meet Again* and Elisabeth Burgos-Debray's *I, Rigoberta Menchú*. Indeed, the Guatemalan testimonial shares the contradictions inherent in Barnet's testimonial piece in that both narratives are framed by the apocalyptic fervor of their times, by what appears to be the last gasp of Western Utopian modernity. In his defense of the *testimonio* as both an ethnographer as well as a writer, Barnet reflects:

> I consider [testimonial novels] as works that have a concrete documentary base in the testimony of the informants interviewed in the course of my work [at the academy of sciences], directed toward a sociological conclusion. That is to say, they are studies of real cases, but recreated, or what might be termed equally, written by me. It is testimony from whose contents I take the juice, the essence, to turn them into fiction and reality. That is why I call them testimonial novels, because the whole historical basis is absolutely trustworthy. I would say that the intention of my books is scientific and literary at the same time. For me, there is no contradiction in this aspect; if I believe I have made a contribution, as some critics have indicated, I think it is in precisely this sense: having been able to create that fusion [of the scientific and the literary]. (Flores 85)

Ethnography, Linguistics, and Narrative Inequality

Why is the witness's speech so uniquely, literally irreplaceable? What does it mean that the testimony cannot simply be reported or narrated by another in its role as testimony? What does it mean that a story—or a history—cannot be told by someone else without forfeiting its unique authenticity, the palpable nature of its reportage? Rather than provide a sense of closure, my concluding remarks will dwell briefly on the directions opened up by the power of language in the testimonial narrative and its implications as words into action outside of the text. In oral cultures repetition is necessary to remember memorable events. Because orality relies on repetition, intellectual experimentation or logical thought is repressed. Orally-based cultures create fluidity, excess, and verbosity that, on another level, function as a smoke screen and, hence, incapacitate important human relations, preventing human beings from recognizing critically certain options for action. Events that are transmitted orally tend to focus on a series of situational moments that fragment experience. Oftentimes, recollected events in individual lives are left without further reflection, without an awareness of their significance for the larger population, without historical context. In testimonial narratives, popular oral elements center the reader in the presentness of the moment, creating a real, immediate, relivable series of cumulative remembered events. Memory is conjured essentially in order to address another, to impress upon a listener, to appeal to a community. The expansion to what we as coerced witnesses can understand in a work of art is due not simply to the impersonal reproduction of events conveyed therein but to the work's power of language, the subtlety of its philosophical and artistic structure, and to the complexity of the creative process it engages. What does testimony mean if it is not simply the observing, the recording, the remembering of an event but an utterly unique and irreplaceable topographical position to an occurrence? What does testimony mean if it is not the uniqueness of the performance of a story which is constituted by the fact that, like the oath, cannot be carried out by anybody else? To testify is not merely to narrate but to commit oneself, and to commit the narrative, to others: to take responsibility—in speech—to history or to the truth of an occurrence for something that goes beyond the personal in having general validity and consequences. The complexity of the relationship between history and witnessing, between art and witnessing is in the power of artistic language not to objectify the event but to both personalize and universalize it to the extent that the text creates a performance response of others outside of the artistic framework. As is the case in a performance text, the testimonial narrative's audience of readers must reflect upon the disjointed voices of the story and arrive at closure regarding the validity and ultimate meaning of the text. In short, the witness empowers the textual recipients with language to understand on an intellectual level, to empathize on an emotional level, but more importantly, to act with a sense of urgency on the sociopolitical level. As a fragment of reality and as a crossroad between art and history, between narrator-interviewer and witness-participant-narrative voice, the testimonial narrative enfolds what is in history untestifiable and embodies, at the same time what in art captures reality and enables witnessing in the first place. In much the same way as the testimonial account, the language of the narrative (oftentimes a blur between the artist and his subject) exemplifies the power of the text to address and hauntingly demands a hearing. We, the recipients of the narrative voice (multiple, collaborative, collective as they may be), are left both empowered and condemned to what is said and what is left unspoken by the *Geheimnisträger,* the "bearers of a secret" never to be divulged.

Notes

1. For a detailed analysis dedicated to testimonial literature as a hybrid genre, refer to John Beverley's essays entitled "The Margin at the Center: On Testimonio (Testimonial Narrative)" in a special issue on Narratives of Colonial Resistance in *Modern Fiction Studies* and his reconsideration of the genre in *Against Literature*.
2. Three relatively recent studies discuss the testimonial narrative in its political context of urgency, particularly in Central America. John Beverley and Marc Zimmerman's collaboration in *Literature and Politics in the Central American Revolutions* provides a compendium and review of the most significant theoretical constructs and historical events linked to literary works in the region. Marc Zimmerman's two-volume text *Literature and Resistance in Guatemala: Textual Modes and Cultural Politics from El Señor Presidente to Rigoberta Menchú* updates the countries by allowing once-silenced voices to speak with authority, with visibility, with the validation of an intellectual counterpart. The dialogic journey of witnessing is motivated by the creation of a communal "we." Last, Linda Craft's *Novels of Testimony and Resistance from Central America* studies the subject from varied perspectives: issues of postmodernism, subalternity, decolonization, nationalism, oral traditions, feminism, and so forth. The emergence of such works from renowned critics in the field attests to both the controversial nature and the literary stature of the genre.
3. In 1986 the Institute for the Studies of Ideologies and Literature, an affiliation of the Society for the Study of Contemporary Hispanic and Lusophone Revolutionary Literatures and the Prisma Institute, published a monograph entitled *Testimonio y literatura,* René Jara and Hernán Vidal, eds., which recognized the genre as a derivation of oral history as witnessing which was once limited to community support networks.
4. In their collaborative work entitled *Testimony. Crises of Witnessing in Literature, Psychoanalysis, and History,* Yale literary critic Shoshana Felman and psychoanalyst Dori Laub examine the nature and function of testimony, witnessing and memory, both in their general relation to the acts of writing and of reading, and in their particular relation to the Holocaust. Their extensive research concludes that it is necessary to speak out about historic traumatic events in order for the reciprocal process of bearing witness and survival to occur.
5. Refer to the extensive bibliographic references in Jane P. Tomkins, *Reader Response Criticism* and the Purdue University Monograph in Romance Languages by Diana Sorensen Goodrich entitled *The Reader and the Text. Interpretive Strategies for Latin American Literatures.*
6. Richard Bauman has studied the linguistic relationship between storytelling in its oral context as well as its transposition in written narrative. For a more detailed analysis, refer to his study on literacy and orality in *Story, Performance, and Event. Contextual Studies of Oral Narrative.*

7. See Ross Chambers's *Story and Situation: Narrative Seduction and the Power of Fiction* and Linda Hutcheon's *Narcissistic Narrative: The Metafictional Paradox*.
8. See Roger Fowler, *Literature as Social Discourse*, Mary Louise Pratt, *Toward a Speech Act Theory of Literary Discourse*, and Barbara Herrnstein Smith, "Narrative Versions, Narrative Theories" in *On Narrative*, edited by W. J. T. Mitchell.
9. See James Olney, *Metaphors of Self: The Meaning of Autobiography*. The Latin American testimonial narrative, although closely resembling the definitions of autobiography set forth in this volume, is unique when it is transcribed from free-flow oral discourse (as opposed to a traditional interview), since it is not always chronological and organized in a cause-effect fashion. See John N. Morris, *Version of the Self* and Roy Pascal, *Design and Truth in Autobiography*.
10. See *I, Rigoberta Menchú. An Indian Woman in Guatemala*. All further references to this source will be indicated in the text. First published in the original Spanish as *Me llamo Rigoberta Menchú y así me nació la conciencia* (Barcelona: Editorial Argos Vergara, 1983).
11. Linguists define substitutionary narration (due to its usual shift in tense and grammatical person) as a "mixture of direct and indirect speech" or "semi-direct" discourse. From the point of view of literary criticism, however, it is better to emphasize what separates the sentence or the lack of a *verbum dicendi* such as "said," "asked," "replied," "declared." In direct as well as indirect discourse, such a verb would indicate that the ensuing words are part of a quotation. In the absence of a *verbum dicendi* and a subordinating conjunction, quoted speech assumes the grammatical disguise of a narrated fact—hence the adequacy of such terms as "veiled speech" and "speech as fact" to the formal characteristics of the sentence.
12. Miguel Barnet lives in Havana, Cuba, where he was born in 1940. He is the acclaimed originator of the tradition of "testimonial" fiction in Latin American letters, and he remains the genre's acknowledged master. Recently he spoke about two of his works (*Akeke* and *La Jutia*) at a conference on Afro-Cubans in Cuba, in Washington D.C. (September 16–17, 1999).

Works Cited

Barnet, Miguel. *Biography of a Runaway Slave.* Trans. W. Nick Hill. Willimantic, CT: Curbstone Press, 1994.
Bauman, Richard. *Story, Performance, and Event. Contextual Studies of Oral Narrative.* Cambridge, UK: Cambridge University Press, 1986.
Beverley, John, and Marc Zimmerman. *Literature and Politics in the Central American Revolutions.* Austin: University of Texas Press, 1990.
Beverley, John. *Against Literature.* Minneapolis: University of Minnesota Press, 1993.
———. "The Margin at the Center: On *Testimonio* (Testimonial Narrative)." *Modern Fiction Studies* (Spring 1989): 11–28.
Castro-Klarén, Sara, Sylvia Molloy, and Beatriz Sario. "Women and Literature in Latin America." *Women's Writing in Latin America. An Anthology.* Westview Press, 1991. 86–87.
Chambers, Ross. *Story and Situation: Narrative Seduction and the Power of Fiction.* Minneapolis: University of Minnesota Press, 1984.
Craft, Linda. *Novels of Testimony and Resistance from Central America.* Gainesville: University Press of Florida, 1997.
Felman, Shoshana, and Dori Laub. *Testimony: Crises of Witnessing in Literature, Psychoanalysis, and History.* New York: Routledge, 1992.
Flores, Angel, ed. *Spanish American Authors: The Twentieth Century.* New York: H. W. Wilson, 1992. 84–86.
Fowler, Roger. *Literature as Social Discourse.* Bloomington: Indiana University Press, 1981.
Goodrich, Diana Sorensen. *The Reader and the Text: Interpretive Strategies for Latin American Literatures.* Philadelphia: John Benjamins, 1986.
Hutcheon, Linda. *Narcissistic Narrative: The Metafictional Paradox.* New York: Methuen, 1984.
Jara, René, and Hernán Vidal, eds. *Testimonio y literatura.* Minneapolis: Prisma, 1986.
Lewis, Oscar. *The Children of Sánchez: Autobiography of a Mexican Family.* New York: Random House, 1961.
Menchú, Rigoberta. *I, Rigoberta Menchú: An Indian Woman in Guatemala.* New York: Verso, 1992.
Morris, John N. *Version of the Self.* New York: Basic Books, 1966.
Olney, James. *Metaphors of Self. The Meaning of Autobiography.* Princeton, NJ: Princeton University Press, 1972.
Pascal, R. *Design and Truth in Autobiography.* Cambridge, MA: Harvard University Press, 1960.
Poniatowska, Elena. "And Here's to You, Jesusa." *Lives on the Line: The Testimony of Contemporary Latin American Authors.* Ed. D. Meyer. Berkeley: University of California Press, 1988. 137–55.
———. *Until We Meet Again.* Trans. Elena Poniatowska. New York: Pantheon Press, 1987.

———. "Women and Literature in Latin America." *Women's Writing in Latin America: An Anthology.* Eds. Sara Castro-Klarén, Sylvia Molloy and Beatriz Sario. Boulder: Westview Press, 1991. 86–87.

Pratt, Mary Louise. *Toward a Speech Act Theory of Literary Discourse.* Bloomington: Indiana University Press, 1977.

Smith, Barbara H. "Narrative Versions, Narrative Theories." Ed. W. J. T. Mitchell. *On Narrative.* Chicago: University of Chicago Press, 1981. 209–32.

Tomkins, Jane P. *Reader Response Criticism* Baltimore: Johns Hopkins University Press, 1980.

Zimmerman, Marc. *Literature and Resistance in Guatemala: Textual Modes and Cultural Politics from El Señor Presidente to Rigoberta Menchú.* Athens: Ohio University Center for International Studies, 1995.

5

On the Trail of an Arctic Tale: Tracing Sir John Franklin in Charles Dickens and Wilkie Collins's *The Frozen Deep*

Erika Behrisch

The Tragic Fall of a Victorian Hero

In the autumn of 1854, Hudson's Bay Company Chief Factor Dr. John Rae delivered to the Admiralty a story, given to him by Inuit hunters, about the mysterious fate of Sir John Franklin's expedition. In 1845, Sir John Franklin had embarked on a three-year journey into the Arctic to discover the Northwest Passage. Until 1854, however—after nineteen searching expeditions had been launched by both Britain and the United States—no information about Franklin's crew had been received, and only the location of their first winter quarters was known.[1] Rae's initial report to the Admiralty, published in *The Times* on October 23 (7a), offered what appeared to be definitive evidence of the expedition's fate. The report recounts "that a party of 'white men' . . . had perished from want of food" a few days away from where Rae had been surveying. Later in the report Rae infers "from the mutilated state of many of the corpses and the contents of the kettles, it is evident that our wretched countrymen had been driven to the last resource—cannibalism—as a means of prolonging existence."[2] Though apparently straightforward and factual, Rae's report understandably met with fierce opposition from the English public. Sir John Franklin was a favorite of the British naval establishment and a national icon, and his expedition had been expected to produce at least some measure of scientific success, though it was unlikely that the entire crew could have survived nine years in the Arctic. Perhaps more importantly, however, as Dickens scholar Ian Stone (1987) succinctly puts it, the prevailing belief was that "Royal naval personnel did not eat each other and that was that" (15). Unexpectedly, Charles

Dickens was one of the most vociferous and vitriolic of Rae's critics, and he used his roles as a creative writer and a celebrity to refute Rae's claims. Rather than merely denounce Rae's report of cannibalism as untrue, however, in his *Household Words* articles Dickens suggests alternate readings of the information Rae's report provides. Dickens goes even further than a mere reinterpretation of Rae's story: In his 1856 production of Wilkie Collins's play, *The Frozen Deep*, I want to argue that Dickens actually enacts a creative retelling of Franklin's fate.

Making History: Victorian Imagination and the Cult of the Explorer

In order to understand fully the significance of Franklin's disappearance (and Arctic exploration in general) to Victorian England, one need only look at the public's perennial interest in the subject. Despite the scarcity of "factual" information on Franklin's whereabouts, essays and opinion papers abounded in the English press, each author offering confident opinions on the probable location of Franklin's crew, its possible discoveries, and its possible fate. Title pieces appeared in such popular social periodicals as *The Athenaeum, Quarterly Review,* and *Fraser's Magazine*, and dailies such as *The Times* and *The Gazette* regularly printed articles and news briefs on the search proceedings. These articles did more than postulate theories; they also served to elevate the character of the Arctic explorer from that of a sailor under the command of the government and science, to that of an inviolable national hero. The man piloting the most extensive expedition and the one most likely to succeed in charting the passage, Franklin was considered the leader of the elite group of Arctic officers, and his character was often used as an illustration of the ideal Victorian man.[3] Just as Franklin's character and fate reflected on the national character, for Victorians the fate of the Franklin expedition was also a national story, a tale in which everyone, as supporters of English exploration and zeal, participated. In his portentously titled *Household Words* article "Unspotted Snow" (1853), Henry Morley sums up the Victorian national interest in Arctic exploration:

> Typhoons, hurricanes, and tropical heats, Inner Africa, Central America, China, Japan, and all such topics interest us; but there are no tales of risk and enterprise in which we English, men, women, and children, old and young, rich and poor, become interested so completely, as in the tales that come from the North Pole. (241)

Morley's enthusiasms about Arctic literature were true: Explorers frequently returned to England and had their journals edited and published for a growing audience. In the age of serialized fiction, the Arctic search for Franklin was just one more story that prolonged suspense, and English audiences waited eagerly for each installment. What Morley does not acknowledge in his article, however, is that most of the stories that "come from the North Pole" were conceived, written, edited, and interpreted in England, and the Arctic and its explorers—and particularly Franklin—thus became mere props for expressing nationalist sentiment.

Though Franklin becomes more interesting as a character in Arctic narrative after his disappearance, before 1845 (the year his last expedition left) he was already established as an author, having published his journals from his 1819 and his 1825 expeditions. Franklin's first text was appreciated for its apparently candid honesty; as Dickens praises the journal in 1854, "The facts are acted and suffered before the reader's eyes" (2 December 1854, *Household* 363).[4] For Dickens, Franklin's adventures comprise a creative performance; the "acting" and the "suffering" in the text are much more valuable than its "facts," and his bias toward the drama of the firsthand tale is a significant element of his critique of Rae's report. According to Dickens, only Franklin can "write the honest story of [his] woes and resignation" (9 December 1854, *Household* 392). At the time of Dickens's writing Franklin had not returned from the Arctic to write his own "honest story," and, therefore, Dickens argued that no one else had proper authority to tell it for him. The natural conclusion to this argument is that any tale that surfaced about Franklin's fate is most likely untrue, particularly any—such as Rae's—which contradicted Franklin's self-definition recorded in his earlier journals.

For Victorians, and for Dickens in particular, Rae's simple tale of cannibalism was impossible to accept; the Arctic explorer, and especially Sir John Franklin was incapable of such an atrocity, and the story must be false. Indeed, Dickens's dismissal of the report as conjecture was, to an extent, supported by Rae's own rhetoric. In his letter to the Admiralty, Rae openly states that the information in his letter was "obtained at various times and from various sources" (7a). Furthermore, Rae admits that "[n]one of the Esquimaux with whom [he] conversed had seen the 'whites.' Nor had they ever been at the place where the bodies were found, but had their information from those who had been there and who had seen the party when traveling" (7a). Though no one was able to prove definitively at the time that Rae's report was false, Rae could not prove it was true, and Dickens denounced the report as a case of irresponsible tale telling.

Canadian storyteller Jan Andrews (5–9) discusses the location of a story as between the teller and the listener. In the case of the Franklin expedition, the space between Rae's report and the public's reception of it was also a site of contention. If the veracity of the Inuit story could be proven, it would significantly alter the heretofore unshaken confidence in the British worldview and would raise "disturbing questions about the traditional faith in British heroism" (Brannan 85). The story's "problematic" origin—problematic because the information was orally transmitted and given in translation—as well as its disturbing implications are the subject of Dickens's initial criticisms. According to Dickens, the "force of [Franklin's] character and discipline, patience and fortitude" evidenced in his earlier journals clearly belies the Inuit tale (2 December 1854, *Household* 363). Franklin's character is set down—by his own hand—in print as "fact," whereas the orally transmitted testimony supported by Rae is nothing more than the "wild tales of a herd of savages" (2 December 1854, *Household* 363). Oral traditions scholar J. Edward Chamberlin (1999) asks the question, "are the 'consequences' of a text ... different depending on whether it is spoken or written?" (69). In Dickens's case, the answer is decidedly yes. In his response to Rae's report, Dickens clearly privileges writing over speech. Furthermore, the distinction between oral conjecture and textual truth also falls along ethnic lines. Specifically, Rae's information is gleaned from a handful of allegedly untrustworthy Natives, whereas Dickens mines endless English and European written accounts for his textual—and therefore "factual"—rebuttal. The fact that Franklin himself is a published author supports Dickens's argument that only Franklin can tell his own tale. Instead of believing the sordid rumors propagated by Natives, Dickens urges the English public to read Franklin's "honest story . . . tenderly and truly in the book he has left us," asserting that Franklin's 1819 journal is a more accurate depiction of his fate than Rae's orally received report (9 December 1854, *Household* 392).[5]

Though Dickens claims in *Household Words* to "thoroughly acquit [Rae] of any trace of blame" for the report (instead blaming the tactless Admiralty for disseminating such a vicious rumor), Rae's enduring faith in Inuit veracity immediately casts doubt on his critical faculties, as Dickens states confidently, "We believe every savage to be in his heart covetous, treacherous, and cruel" (2 December 1854, *Household* 361, 362). Dickens's animadversions on the "vague babble" of the natives is by no means unusual (2 December 1854, *Household* 365). For example, the *North British Review* in 1851 published a succinct footnote to its article on the Franklin searches. It states, "the testimony of the Natives cannot be trusted . . . the coast is 'alive' with stories concerning the missing crews, and . . . the Esquimaux are ever ready to exercise their ingenuity by inventing a story" (468). In their own essays about Franklin's fate, however, English writers were just as willing to "invent a story," so long as it had an ending copacetic with their cultural assumptions of what was acceptable. In *Household Words*, Dickens goes so far as to provide his readers with a variety of alternative endings to Franklin's saga, all based on his opinions of both the role of the Inuit and of the British navigator in the Arctic. At various points in his argument, Dickens accuses Rae's Inuit informants of lying either for possible gain or out of guilt for having stolen material from the missing ships. He accuses Rae's interpreter of grossly exaggerating in order to impress his employer. The rest of the "herd of savages" he accuses of nothing less than Franklin's murder.

Despite his eloquent slandering of the Inuit character, however, I would argue that Dickens's ethnocentric defense of Franklin has more to do with his faith in the British naval officer than with his distrust of Arctic Natives. Rejecting Inuit testimony as false is only one way for Dickens to argue that British sailors, in whatever state of exigency, would not resort to cannibalism. Dickens's main defense of Franklin lies actually in his lengthy catalogue of historical shipwrecks and the behavior of other—European—crews. This defense Dickens terms "close analogy," and in it he compares Franklin's behavior on his past Arctic voyages to the behavior of other less disciplined crews (2 December 1854, *Household* 361). According to Dickens, Franklin's crew was made up of "seamen of the first class," hand-picked from the elite of the British navy (2 December 1854, *Household* 363). The characters of these men Dickens sets in opposition to historical accounts of crews who are known to have resorted to cannibalism, and Dickens points out that these acts are perpetrated either by foreign sailors, or by men he "confidently [assumes] . . . to have been of an inferior class" (9 December 1854, *Household* 387). As in his rejection of Inuit testimony, Dickens's conclusions here are admittedly also culturally grounded. However, his conclusions reflect more upon Franklin than upon those with whom he is favorably compared, underlining Franklin as the subject of discussion, not European cannibals or Inuit informants. Dickens's conclusion to his cannibal analogy is, "the better educated the man, the better disciplined the habits, the more reflective and religious the tone of thought, the more gigantically improbable the 'last resource' becomes" (2 December 1854, *Household* 365). For Franklin, an Englishman, a rear admiral, and a deeply religious man knighted by Queen Victoria, cannibalism is clearly not an option.[6]

Just as Dickens rejects Rae's report as a badly constructed and exaggerated tale, however, Dickens's own article disintegrates under the same criticism. In his prompt response to Dickens in *Household Words*, Rae points out that "One or two facts are worth a hundred theories on any subject" (23 December 1854, *Household* 434). Rae then proceeds to dismantle Dickens's argument in the same manner in which Dickens attacks his, drawing on the "facts" at his fingertips: his own experience of the Arctic and his relationships with both Inuit and English. For example, while Dickens expounds the virtues of Franklin's hand-picked crew, Rae observes that "their conduct at the very last British port they entered was not such as to make those who knew it, consider them very deserving of the high eulogium passed upon them in *Household Words*" (30 December 1854, *Household* 458). Though bad conduct at a port of sailing is certainly no measure of a crew's propensity for cannibalism, Rae's inclusion of small facts such as this implies Dickens's rhetoric is much dramatic puffery, with little weight behind it. Furthermore, Dickens's references are, like Rae's, "obtained at various times and from various sources." His examples of crews' cannibalistic behavior are gleaned from official reports and edited journals, narratives from as early as the sixteenth century, and literary translations of older foreign texts. Dickens's own refutation of Rae's report is itself a "very unsatisfactory document on which to found such strong conclusions as it takes for granted" (Dickens 3 February 1855, *Household* 12).

Remaking History: Staging Alternatives to Disaster

In 1856, after Rae's effective rebuttal to his arguments in *Household Words*, Dickens commissioned Wilkie Collins to script *The Frozen Deep*.[7] Set in the Arctic and dealing with the theme of man's struggle to maintain honor and integrity under duress, I want to argue that *The Frozen Deep* is Dickens's final, allegorical defense of Franklin's character against Rae's report. Robert Brannan (1966) claims that "The Arctic expedition in *The Frozen Deep* was associated with the Franklin expedition, though not identified with it" (85). In reading Dickens's *Household Words* articles in conjunction with *The Frozen Deep*, however, the play invites a much closer identification with the Franklin expedition than Victorian and contemporary critics either notice or admit. The fact that

Dickens invited important members of Parliament and well-known dramatic critics—not to mention Queen Victoria—to attend suggests that he had political motivations for producing it, and its obvious allusions to the lost expedition support the theory that the play is a revision of the Franklin tale. Certainly Dickens is under no illusions about Franklin's death; in his prologue to the play he introduces the setting as the place "Where PARRY conquer'd and FRANKLIN died," and the play does not even attempt to suggest that survivors of the expedition exist (97).[8] The play does, however, offer a radical revisioning of how Franklin was perceived after Rae's report, implying that the doubt cast upon his character by the charge of cannibalism is thoroughly unwarranted.

The villain-cum-hero of the play—whom I would call Dickens's dramatic representation of Franklin—is Richard Wardour, a Royal naval officer whose expedition is missing in the Arctic, living to revenge himself upon the man who stole his beloved. The lover who has rejected him is Clara Burnham, an impressionable young lady greatly under the influence of her Scottish Nurse Esther, who claims the gift of Second Sight and continually prophesies doom for Wardour's expedition. Clara's fiancé, Frank Aldersley, also a Royal Naval officer, is a member of Wardour's missing expedition and is unaware of Wardour's designs on his life. The play enacts the tale of Wardour's initial quest for revenge, his identification of Frank Aldersley as his archenemy, his apparent triumph as he disappears with Frank into a snowstorm, and his eventual return to civilization to deliver a weakened Frank into Clara's arms, clear his name from the suspicion of murder, and die a noble death.

As in Dickens's *Household Words* defense of Franklin, *The Frozen Deep* also uses "close analogy" to make its point. The context of the play draws heavily on the facts of the first and the last Franklin expeditions: Franklin's missing ships, the *Erebus* and *Terror*, victualed for three years, are obvious models for the play's two vessels, victualed for the same time and equally lost in the Arctic. The hut the men use for shelter is reminiscent of a hut constructed by Franklin in his 1819 journal, which, as previously mentioned, was so highly praised by Dickens. *The Frozen Deep*, however, also has many significant deviations. The play's Arctic scenes of starvation remain dignified, and the possibility of cannibalism is completely removed. For example, in Franklin's account of his 1819 journey, he and his men are reduced to eating poisonous lichen, roasted shoe leather and "the scraps of acrid marrow yet remaining in the dried and whitened spines of dead wolves" (Dickens, 2 December 1854, *Household* 362). In *The Frozen Deep*, however, though there is no food, mealtime still occurs with the regularity of a well-run country kitchen, and the grumbling but good-natured cook sets to work with his mortar and pestle to grind bone soup for the officers and men. More importantly, in Richard Wardour's quest to avenge his broken heart, the specter of cannibalism that hangs over the real expedition becomes instead a classic tale of rejected love and revenge.

Brannan gives this reason for the absence of cannibalism in *The Frozen Deep*: It was "suited neither to Tavistock House at Christmas time nor to a character whose role Dickens was to play" (85). However, the absence of cannibalism in the play is more significant; it supports Dickens's argument in *Household Words* that it did not exist at all. In heightening the revenge context of the play's expedition, Dickens draws attention away from the subtext of cannibalism and directs it instead to the social drama of Richard Wardour's moral struggle. Thus, as Richard Wardour leaves on his trek with Frank Aldersley, the threat is one of passionate murder, not cannibalism. The drama is then still socially grounded: Aldersley represents not a portable food source but the source of Wardour's broken heart. Indeed, Aldersley is valuable to Wardour only if he remains alive, so Wardour can exact his revenge.

As a rewriting of Franklin's end, *The Frozen Deep* is in direct contrast to what Dickens terms Rae's "incoherent Esquimaux story" (2 December 1854, *Household* 362). The conspicuous absence of any Native character in the play highlights the author's absolute rejection of Rae's report. Inuit are not even given representation in *The Frozen Deep*, let alone given a chance to speak. Indeed, the play expresses from first to last a sort of ethnic anxiety and fear of cultural infiltration: The safe English community—both in England and in the Arctic—can exist only if each character abides by the domestic rules of conduct. Introduced in Act II as the play's villain, Wardour exhibits extreme antisocial tendencies, which both exclude him from the supportive community of his fellow sailors and also imply his capacity for murder, the ultimate antisocial act. The cultural insularity and strong sense of community established in the first Act are essential for the enactment of the play's fantasy: The English are capable of looking after their own, and any foreign interference is always detrimental. For instance, Clara Burnham, the play's delicate heroine, remains isolated from the safety of her English friends by hostile and foreign interlopers because her "mother... has gone abroad, and married again [and] has never forgiven Clara for objecting to a foreign Stepfather" (*Frozen* Act I, 102). More important, however, is the presence of Clara's Scottish Nurse Esther, who has a peculiar hold over Clara's nerves and sanity and continually prophesies the expedition's doom.

However, because of her role as doomsayer of the expedition, I want to argue that Nurse Esther is Dickens's representation of Dr. Rae and his "tale-telling Inuit." Born in the north of Scotland and educated in Edinburgh, Rae seems a likely model for the Highland-born and Lowland-educated Nurse Esther. Furthermore, Esther's predictions of Frank Aldersley's death are reminiscent of Rae's report to the Admiralty (dramatic license aside). Fitted with an accent that places her at least one social level below the other ladies of the play, Esther believes in the Second Sight, and she claims to act as a conduit for other voices, who can see and predict the fate of the missing expedition. However, the possibility remains that her prophesies are nothing more than shrewd guesses and piecings together of information she has overheard; when Esther tells Clara that "the stain o' [Frank Aldersley's] bluid" is upon her for not telling him of Wardour's threat, the audience knows Esther has overheard Clara speaking of Frank's danger and may possibly be using Clara's vulnerability to her own ends, much as Dickens suspects the Inuit of doing to Rae, and Rae of possibly doing to the English public (116).[9] The reference to Rae and his faith in Inuit testimony again becomes explicit in the rescued sailors' dismissal of Esther in Act III: "No woman but a Scotch woman would set any vally by a second hand eye" (146). Like the subject of Rae's report, "obtained at various times and from various sources," Esther's Second Sight is "mostly made up of bits that she picked up here, and bits that she picked up there; and then she goes and pieces them together, sometimes right and oftener wrong, and then forgets she did it, being a Muddle-headed female, and sets up for a prophet" (146).

Rediscovering Lost Heroes

The play's final Act comprises Dickens's most substantial revision of Franklin's story, enacting fantasies of rescue, the heroic return of the "intrepid sailors" (as the men from Franklin's ships were popularly known in the press), and the vindication of Wardour's name from the charge of murder. Though all of the Admiralty's search expeditions for Franklin were unsuccessful, the men in *The Frozen Deep* are rescued by the government's timely first attempt, and the last act is set on the coast of Newfoundland, where the rescued sailors rest for their journey home. In a well-placed conversation with the cook, who no longer serves pounded bone soup but lays a table for a hearty feast, an officer explains, "we were saved from starving and freezing to death by a searching expedition from England, which discovered us in that Arctic hut of ours" (147). Thus in the play's reenactment, the British government's efforts are successful, restoring the audience's faith in Britain's ability to make good pledges and reestablishing the Arctic navigator in a seat of honor. Also, of course, in the final act Nurse Esther's repeated convictions that Richard Wardour has killed Frank Aldersley are proven wrong. Just as Franklin is incapable of committing cannibalism because of his character, as a gentleman, Wardour is incapable of killing for revenge. By analogy, Wardour's return and vindication argue that Franklin's physical presence is necessary in order to learn the true story of his expedition's fate. When Wardour disappears, his companions mistakenly assume the worst of his character, and he becomes the play's villain. Only by reappearing at the end and proving his accusers wrong does Wardour become the play's hero. The play urges its audience not to make the same mistake twice but to suspend their judgment on Franklin until more definitive evidence is discovered that will prove him, of course, innocent. Because Franklin is unable to make a heroic return to England to clear his own name, the charge of cannibalism laid upon him by Rae's report should be dismissed, like Nurse Esther's faulty Second Sight, as a case of false prophesying.

Ironically, Dickens's portrayal of Wardour as the villain cum hero is somewhat prophetic in itself. Fourteen years after his disappearance, in 1859—metaphorically the last act of the Franklin drama—Franklin was exonerated from the charge of cannibalism. A paper recording his death in 1847 proved he had died before his men were forced to leave their ships. The doubt thrown on Richard Wardour's character until the end of the play when he returns to tell his own story parallels Franklin's situation, exacerbated by Rae's report. Wardour's miraculous return is no coincidence. Like Franklin, only he can return to tell his own "honest story."

Notes

1. There are numerous reconstructions of the movements and fate of the Franklin expedition, both from Victorian times and from the present. For a contemporary's published journal of an early search, see Sherard Osborn, *Stray Leaves from an Arctic Journal* (1852); for a general account of England's reaction to Franklin's disappearance, I recommend Pierre Berton's *The Arctic Grail* (chap. four) (1988); for the fascinating (if morbid) details of the expedition's last days, see Owen Beattie and John Geiger, *Frozen in Time* (1987).
2. Rae's report appears in full in the British House of Lords Sessional Papers (1854–55), vol. x: 879–97. It was also printed by Dickens in *Household Words* 254 (3 February 1855):12–20.
3. Sir John Franklin was a favorite subject in published poems and Victorian ballads and was frequently mentioned in Victorian dailies, literary magazines, and in Parliament as "heroic, " "intrepid, " and "dauntless"; in his absence representations of his character very likely exceeded reality.
4. Perhaps for continuity purposes, the majority of Dickens's articles on Franklin are titled, "The Lost Arctic Voyagers." I have used publication dates to identify each article from *Household Words*.
5. This privileging of written evidence over oral testimony still continues; Edward Parkinson pieces together the trials of Franklin's men by extrapolating from the few pieces of written material that have survived since the expedition's disappearance (one scrap of paper and one official report). See Edward Parkinson (1997), "'All Well': Narrating the Third Franklin Expedition." In *Echoing Silence*, ed. John Moss, 43–52. David C. Woodman, however, does much to credit Inuit oral testimony in piecing together the details of the Franklin disaster. See David Woodman (1997), "Inuit Accounts and the Franklin Mystery." In *Echoing Silence*, ed. John Moss. 53–60; and David Woodman (1995), *Strangers Among Us*.
6. Ian Stone makes the observation that, contrary to Dickens's opinion, "cannibalism at sea does seem to have been not infrequent" in the nineteenth century and earlier (11). Despite Dickens's assertions to the contrary, his own surfeit of examples of cannibalism in *Household Words* supports this.
7. *The Frozen Deep* is a Christmas play written by Collins for Dickens's annual Tavistock House productions. Collins, then a young and unsuccessful novelist newly hired for *Household Words*, was specifically commissioned by Dickens to write a tragedy set in the Arctic. After Collins finished the script, Dickens substantially revised it and is now commonly identified as the major contributor.
8. Though Dickens extensively reworks the Franklin tale, his acceptance of Franklin's death remains. In 1856 and 1857, however, this opinion was not yet universal, and members of the British and American scientific communities—and Lady Franklin—were still urging the Admiralty to conduct a search for possible survivors.

9. Rae was awarded £10,000 for his report to the Admiralty, in spite of the fact that he had not visited the site himself. According to the Admiralty, the relics Rae had purchased from his Native informants (crested spoons, buttons, and so forth) were enough to provide definitive evidence that his report was true (it was eventually verified by Captain McClintock in 1859). Rae initially claimed to be unaware of the reward offered (it was announced in the papers in 1850), but then wrote several letters to the Admiralty on his own behalf regarding the adjudication of the reward. See British House of Lords Sessional Papers (1856), vol. x: 355.

Works Cited

Andrews, Jan. "The Space Between." *Appleseed Quarterly: The Canadian Journal of Storytelling* 8.1 (1998): 5–9.

"The Arctic Expedition." *The Times* (23 October 1854): 7a.

"Arctic Searching Expeditions." *North British Review* 16 (1851–1852): 445–91.

Beattie, Owen, and John Geiger. *Frozen in Time: Unlocking the Secrets of the Franklin Expedition.* Saskatoon: Western Producer Prairie Books, 1987.

Berton, Pierre. *The Arctic Grail: The Quest for the North West Passage and the North Pole 1818–1909.* Toronto: McClelland and Stewart, 1988.

Brannan, Robert. *Under the Management of Charles Dickens, His Production of* The Frozen Deep. New York: Cornell University Press, 1966.

British House of Lords Sessional Papers. 1856. Vol. X:355.

Chamberlin, J. Edward. "Doing Things with Words: Putting Performance on the Page." *Talking on the Page.* Eds. Laura Murray and Keren Rice. Toronto: Toronto University Press, 1999. 69–90.

Collins, Wilkie, and Charles Dickens. *The Frozen Deep.* 1856. *Under the Management of Charles Dickens, His Production of "The Frozen Deep."* Ed. Robert Brannan. New York: Cornell University Press, 1966. 97–156.

Dickens, Charles. "The Lost Arctic Voyagers." *Household Words* 245 (2 December 1854): 361–65.

———. "The Lost Arctic Voyagers." *Household Words* 246 (9 December 1854): 386–93.

———. "Prologue to *The Frozen Deep.*" 1856. *Under the Management of Charles Dickens, His Production of* "The Frozen Deep." Ed. Robert Brannan. New York: Cornell University Press, 1966. 97.

———. "Sir John Franklin and His Crews." *Household Words* 254 (3 February 1855): 12–20.

Morley, Henry. "Unspotted Snow." *Household Words* 190 (12 November 1853): 241–46.

Osborn, Sherard. *Stray Leaves from an Arctic Journal.* London: Longmans, 1852.

Parkinson, Edward. "'All Well': Narrating the Third Franklin Expedition." *Echoing Silence: Essays on Arctic Narrative.* Ed. John Moss. Ottawa: University of Ottawa Press, 1997. 43–52.

Rae, John. "Dr. Rae's Report." *Household Words* 249 (30 December 1854): 457–59.

———. Letter to the Secretary of the Admiralty. *The Times* (23 October 1854): 7a.

———. "The Lost Arctic Voyagers." *Household Words* 248 (23 December 1854): 433–37.

Stone, Ian."'The Contents of the Kettles': Charles Dickens, John Rae and Cannibalism on the 1845 Franklin Expedition." *The Dickensian* 83. 1 (411) (spring 1987): 6–16.

Woodman, David C. "Inuit Accounts and the Franklin Mystery." *Echoing Silence: Essays on Arctic Narrative*. Ed. John Moss. Ottawa: University of Ottawa Press, 1997. 53–60.
———. *Strangers Among Us*. Montreal: McGill-Queen's University Press, 1995.

6

Constructing the Witch

Karen Seago

Since the seventies, the work of feminist critics has drawn attention to and analyzed the restricted gender roles fairy tales offer as role models to children. Studies have shown how gender-specific behavior is encoded into classic stories whose clearly enunciated framework of good and evil socializes children into ideologically inflected norms of femininity and masculinity.[1] These reward passivity, beauty, and suffering as female virtues and identify most forms of activity, intellectual, physical, or sexual power and attempts at self-determination as negatively inflected features when linked to a female character. Most importantly, female relationships are structured by jealousy and competition for male recognition and reward. Thus, the classic fairy-tale heroine is usually persecuted by a female competitor, often an older woman, and saved by a prince figure.[2]

Sleeping Beauty is often cited as the archetypal fairy tale and in popular, Anglo-American reception the story certainly conforms to the paradigm of innocence, persecution, and a clearly articulated dichotomy of good and evil. The storyline of the young princess cursed by an older woman with evil intent is most clearly developed in Disney's film, in which the femme-fatale-witch engages in an elaborately drawn-out persecution of the innocent princess. The story ends up in a battle between the witch and the savior prince. This confrontation develops into an allegory of the fight of good vs. evil in explicitly Christian terms. Much critical attention has been paid to the role of the innocent persecuted heroine (Bacchilega *Perspectives*), but in this paper I wish to concentrate on the role of the older, persecuting woman in *Sleeping Beauty*. Relating the classic story to its sources and in particular its grounding in myth, I will analyze how the figure of the witch is constructed in dominant reception and how the character comes to express cultural anxiety over the unmarried woman.

The Anglo-American version of *Sleeping Beauty* is based on two European traditions: Charles Perrault's late seventeenth-century version, *La Belle au bois dormant*, and the German story, *Dornröschen* collected by the Brothers Grimm in the early nineteenth century. In 1729, Robert Samber had translated Perrault into English, and the story was extremely popular in chapbook format. However, it was the translation of the German version by Taylor in 1823, which ultimately helped establish the fairy tale as acceptable children's reading in England. The Grimms' tales were cited by authors arguing for and defending the moral value of traditional stories as appropriately educational reading throughout the century. That the influential cultural critic John Ruskin wrote a respectful introduction to an 1868 edition of the tales is an indication of the high value placed on the Grimm tales. Thus, for much of the nineteenth century, the German tradition dominated the English translations aimed at the children's literature market. However, in the case of *Sleeping Beauty*, in the course of the century, elements from the French tradition were increasingly incorporated and further developed to form the canonic tale. I believe that this merging took place because the German version of *Sleeping Beauty* was far more ambiguous in its value system, less clear cut in its representation of the figure of the surplus fairy, and not as judgmental as the French-derived versions.

The differences in the representation of the "witch-figure" between the two traditions are as follows. In Perrault's elegant, aristocratic version, seven fairies are invited to the christening feast because the eighth, and oldest, fairy has withdrawn from society and cannot be traced. Nevertheless, she appears at the baptism and is annoyed that her table setting is less precious than those of the other fairies. Her spiteful mumbling is observed by the youngest fairy, who hides herself toward the end of the meal, anticipating mischief. When the oldest fairy duly curses the child with death, the youngest still has her blessing and can use it to mitigate the curse to a 100-year sleep and rescue by a prince. In the French version, the surplus fairy is responsible for her exclusion from the feast because she had removed herself from society, and her character is clearly unpleasant: She is explicitly portrayed as old and spiteful, which further justifies her exclusion. This is not the case in the German tradition where the thirteenth fairy is excluded by chance and human fallibility because the King has only twelve golden plates, and therefore he only invites twelve fairies. The exclusion is not the surplus fairy's fault, it does not lie in her character; she could be any one of the thirteen, and she reacts to the slight by turning up at the end of the celebrations when the other fairies are almost done blessing the child. Clearly explaining herself and identifying her action as a punishment for the exclusion, she curses the child with death. This is mitigated not by design (as it is in the French version) but by chance: The thirteenth fairy arrived before the last of the fairies had blessed the child; she (the last fairy) therefore uses her good wish to turn the curse of death into a 100-year sleep.

However, while the French tale shows some of the motifs relevant for today's story (namely the young-old dichotomy, the spiteful nature of the old fairy, and the fact that she is herself responsible for her exclusion) neither the French nor the German version has a fully developed witch-figure in the sense that there is no planning and no intentional persecution of the princess. In both versions, the curse is a response to the exclusion, and that it is the princess who suffers is incidental. The excluded fairy merely sets into motion the main plot development but then disappears from the story. The old woman whose spindle brings about the fulfillment of the curse is not linked to the witch figure but is portrayed in a neutral way, and in the French tradition she is positively helpful. In this, both traditions are still recognizably influenced by the story's mythic sources.

Although the storyline of *Sleeping Beauty* is dependent on literary tradition (see Opie and Opie 102–8), there are two strands of mythic and mytho-literary derivation based in Greek and Nordic myth, which have contributed to the plot structure of *Sleeping Beauty*. One strand provides the basis for the motif cluster of blessing-curse-mitigation, while the other strand accounts for the sleep (as punishment)-male awakening presence (kiss)-persecution configuration.

The core motifs of blessing, curse, and mitigation can be traced to the three Fates or Norns, goddesses in Greek and Nordic myth, who spin the thread of life: One is responsible for the beginning of life, one ensures maturity, and the third cuts off the thread of life, representing death. This myth was popularized in oral stories, extant in medieval source books where the Fates or Norns are represented as traveling fairies, magicians or wise women who attend celebrations of birth and bless the child with their gifts—and where the gift of death is explained as a curse, which then is, fortunately, mitigated by the other Fates—instant death is delayed (Grimm *Mythologie* 228–36 and *Schriften* 191–201).

The second strand of mytho-literary derivation providing the more complex motif configuration of sleep (as punishment)—male awakening presence (kiss)—persecution is the Nordic myth of Odin and Brünhilde, developed variously in the Middle High German *Nibelungenlied*, the Norse *Edda*, the *Völsungasaga*, and *Thidrekssaga* (Romain). Odin curses his daughter, the bravest of all valkyries, with sleep as a punishment for infringing his authority. In response to her pleas, he mitigates his humiliating decision that she should be woken and become the wife of the first man to pass by, so that only the bravest of all men, able to pass through the ring of flames (swords) surrounding her, should claim her. However, Siegfried achieves this feat and claims Brünhilde as wife for his lord Gunther, who is himself not able to do so. In a quarrel between Siegfried's wife Krimhild and Brünhilde, Krimhild taunts (persecutes) her rival with having been Siegfried's whore. This strand applies in different ways to the French and the German tradition, and its relevance to the development of the persecutory witch will be discussed toward the end of this essay.

While the first strand of mythic-oral mediation is relevant for both traditions, it is particularly prominent in the German tradition, where the three roles are more clearly demarcated than in the French: The role of the Fate or Norn responsible for birth is enacted in the Grimm version by a crab, later a frog, who shares a bath with the queen and prophesies the birth of a much-desired child. The fairies invited to the birthday celebration of the princess bestow their magical gifts and fulfill the role of ensuring a prosperous life, whereas the excluded fairy plays the role of the third Fate with her "curse" of death. Even the motif of the slight can be traced. In some medieval stories, the third Fate's gift of death is presented as an angry response—the third Fate or Norn was accidentally tripped up, fell off her chair, or was not given a knife (Grimm *Mythology* 1401). Thus the inevitability of death is explained by inserting it into a human framework of emotional cause and effect. There is a difference, though, between this mythic representation and the spiteful fairy in Perrault or later mediations of the story. Despite the apparent tit-for-tat reaction in the medieval story, the mythic is not interested in a prescriptive didactic representation but is a contemplation of the human condition. Emotional reactions such as anger are an attempt to comprehend the fact of death but do not function within a judgmental framework: There is no reward-punishment scheme linked to desirable behavior as we find in the classic fairy story.

The complete *Kinder- und Hausmärchen* had seven editions between 1812 and 1857, and the selected "small edition" ran to ten editions between 1825 and 1857. Wilhelm Grimm continued editing these throughout, and his alterations to the corpus of tales and to the texts of individual stories are well documented (Schoof, Rölleke, "Biographie" and "Nachwort," Tatar, Bottigheimer). However, due to the brothers' political motivation of proving their collection of tales to be evidence of an ancient German mythically derived literature (Seitz, Kamenetsky), the early Grimm editions are at pains to remain close to the mythic/medieval sources in their portrayal of the thirteenth fairy and the curse as fate; as with the three Fates or Norns, she is in no way singled out but is part of the community of fairies. Furthermore, her reaction is not condemned but presented as a justified punishment, which recalls Odin's punishment of Brünhilde. Wilhelm Grimm foregrounded the mythic character of the fairies in the second edition of 1819 by referring to them as "wise women," giving them the status of (half-) gods in Nordic myth. Importantly, the thirteenth is not explicitly excluded from this descriptor and remains by implication a "wise woman" throughout. Nevertheless, Wilhelm's continued editorial interventions affected the representation of the thirteenth "wise woman" so that by the last edition of 1857 she had lost much of her mythic impartiality and power, and her justified anger had become a transgression of bourgeois codes of conduct.

In the first edition of 1812, the thirteenth fairy gives a reason for her behavior, identifying it as a punishment for her exclusion, and her direct speech is identified as the language of prophecy *ich verkündige euch* (I prophesy you). In the second edition, Wilhelm removes the thirteenth fairy's own explanation of her action. The narratorial voice instead interprets her motivation as revenge rather than justified punishment, thus losing the link to Odin's anger. In addition, the thirteenth fairy's direct speech now only consists of the curse, resulting in a loss of rational characterization and the association with prophetic language is replaced with the more emotive *Sie rief* (She called out). Her heightened emotional state is further foregrounded in 1840 and again in 1850 when Wilhelm adds descriptions of her behavior which becomes increasingly offensive; she enters without greeting anybody or looking at them; she shouts in a loud voice and abruptly rushes out without saying anything else after she has cursed the child:

> da trat plötzlich die dreizehnte herein. Sie wollte sich dafür rächen, daß sie nicht eingeladen war, und ohne jemand zu grüßen und anzusehen,

rief sie mit lauter Stimme "die Königstocher . . ." Nach diesen Worten kehrte sie sich um und verließ den Saal.

Suddenly the thirteenth entered. She wanted to revenge herself for the fact that she had not been invited, and without greeting anybody or looking at them, she called out in a loud voice "the king's daughter . . ." After these words she turned around and left the hall. (1850)

The character traits of impatience, arrogance, and a temper the thirteenth fairy acquires in the course of editorial changes, are identified in contemporary conduct manuals as those that will endanger a girl's chances of catching a husband (Held 108–51, Duden 125–40, especially 137). The thirteenth fairy thus provides a warning foil for the princess's good behavior. All the virtues the girl had been blessed with by the other wise women, and of which we are assured explicitly in the text (1850) that they are fulfilled and make the princess beloved of everybody, are specifically named in conduct manuals as positive character traits, e.g., those that will lead to marriage:

An dem Mädchen aber wurden die Gaben der weisen Frauen sämmtlich erfüllt, denn es war so schön, sittsam, freundlich und verständig, daß es jedermann, der es ansah, lieb haben mußte.

But in the girl all the gifts of the wise women came true, since she was so beautiful, virtuous, friendly and understanding that anybody who looked on her, had to love her. (1850)

In addition, the negative characterization of the thirteenth fairy not only functions in relation to the portrayal of the princess but also has an effect on the representation of the king. Because he had decided not to invite the thirteenth wise woman—because there were not enough plates—he was responsible for the curse on his child. This element was not changed in Wilhelm's editing, but with the increasingly offensive behavior of the thirteenth fairy, an indirect exoneration of the king's behavior is effected, justifying his decision to exclude her in a way similar to the motivation in Perrault's version. Nevertheless, despite these revisions, the German texts still retain elements of the mythic context that do not allow a full exclusion and demonization of the thirteenth fairy, and there is no indication of the good-evil or young-old dichotomies.

The elements introduced by Wilhelm's editorial revision, namely the indirect exoneration of the king which shifts responsibility for her exclusion to the thirteenth fairy, her offensive and unjustified behavior, and the beginnings of a judgmental attitude, are taken up and developed in

English translations between 1823 and 1888 (Taylor 1823 and 1839, Wehnert, Davis, Gillies, Paull, Crane, Hunt, Gardiner).

Adaptation into the context of children's literature further contributed to textual strategies with a socializing and prescriptively didactic impetus where the explicit articulation of good and evil became closely linked to emerging notions of manliness and femininity. The king's behavior is adapted in translation to operate as a model of rational decision making, wisdom, and controlled emotions, all traits of manliness foregrounded from mid-century (Nelson 534–36). He is also a responsible father, who is not implicated in the decision to exclude the thirteenth fairy or who does not leave his child on her fifteenth birthday as the German king and queen do. In addition to the indirect shifting of blame, which the Grimm source texts had initiated, various textual strategies are employed to exonerate the king from responsibility directly, and the already bad behavior of the thirteenth fairy is further exaggerated, thus polarizing exemplary male behavior and female transgression even more sharply.

With the exception of Taylor's first translation in 1823 and Hunt's definitive translation in 1884, all of the texts I analyzed introduce in varying degree the good-evil dichotomy in their treatment of the fairies by adding descriptors such as "good" (Paull 193), "benevolent" (Gillies 284), "friendly" (Taylor *German Popular Stories and Fairy Tales* 27), "kind and well-inclined to children" (Davis 193) and "kind and good" (Taylor *German Popular Stories and Fairy Tales* 26) to the 12 invited fairies; and "evil" (Gillies 285), "spiteful" (Gillies 284) and "bad" (Paull 194), and "wicked" (Paull 193, 196) to the thirteenth fairy. Taylor's substantially revised 1839 translation is particularly explicit by introducing an elaborate iconography of differentiated clothing and attributes for the "friendly" fairies who wear red clothes and carry white wands while the thirteenth fairy is clearly identified through her black clothing and the attributes of the witch because she carries a broomstick and wears a high black cap (27). Whereas other translations do not take this element up in their textual treatment, it is nevertheless carried over into paratextual elements, such as illustrations.

In contrast to the German source texts where the unity of the thirteenth fairy is implicitly maintained, the English translations are intent on dissociating the thirteenth fairy from the other fairies. She is the threatening outsider who disrupts the social fabric, while the good fairies are integrated into human society. However, their power is reduced, domesticated, and firmly aligned with the private sphere and the family.

Most texts do not refer to them as "wise women" but as fairies, which in the nineteenth century had a strong association with diminutive size and scope. Where the application of "wise women" is retained in 1853 (Wehnert 243, 244), it is interpreted within the domestic ideal as caring and nurturing with a special affinity to children (244). In an 1855 text, the mitigation is even cast in the language of the nursery, describing the power to avert death as "applying a remedy against the effect of the 13th fairy's decree" (Davis 193–94).

Thus, the good fairies are assimilated into the domestic setting while the thirteenth fairy comes to stand for deviating forms of femininity. Showing typical characteristics of the bad, or fallen woman, she is noisy which was seen as a sign of moral collapse, and her loud protest further compromises her: In popular articles and medical discourse a loud, harsh, or hoarse voice was identified as one of the attributes by which a prostitute could be recognized (Matus 48–49). In the 1850s and 1860s, great anxiety existed over the explosion of the "social evil" of prostitution, which was seen as a "street disorder" threatening to infect "healthy areas" (Walkowitz 41). In fact, translations in the 1850s and 1860s show similar anxieties in their concern over how to identify the bad woman and exclude her polluting influence.

The thirteenth fairy is angry and transgresses accepted codes of social conduct by acting in exactly the opposite way to how women were counseled to behave even when wronged. Influential conduct writers state that "an enraged woman is one of the most disgusting sights in nature" (Chapone 45), and advise that woman demonstrates her "rational being" by remaining silent and meek in an argument, bearing "provocation" with "equanimity" (Freeling 32). The thirteenth fairy is delegitimated in a double move by texts that ridicule her anger by translating it as a trivial "affront" (Davis 193) or as "disrespect" (Gillies 284) and at the same time emphasizing her reaction to the slight as exaggerated and inappropriate: she is "greatly incensed" (Gillies 284), in a "tremendous passion" (Wehnert 244), "burning to revenge herself" (Crane 204). Her social exclusion and ostracism are legitimated by presenting it as the outcome of her own behavior. She has placed herself outside the community by offending repeatedly against the rules of seemly womanhood when she not only complains about an injustice but when textual strategies imply that this "injustice" "objectively" does not exist. In effect, she is making a fuss over nothing, an established strategy by dominant ideology to invalidate protests against its exclusions.

The dissociation of the thirteenth fairy from the rest of the fairies also identifies her as a single woman, a figure of great anxiety from the mid-nineteenth century. The 1851 census had provided statistical evidence of the surplus of women and initiated the fiercely debated "Woman Question." Countless articles, primarily in the 1860s, discussed what was to be done with the 'dangerous' surplus of women (Palmegiano 70–95). The "odd woman," as she was known, was treated with pity and contempt, but she was also considered a social failure and was regarded with distrust. Whereas ideological constructions of gender insisted on a complementary nature of the sexes, unmarried women posed a problem because their single state barred them from fulfilling their maternal role which their instinct and their nature assigned them, thus making them unnatural and deviant (Poovey 4). The unmarried, or unmarriageable, spinster disrupts and threatens the stable unit of the couple and the family, like the witch disturbing the ceremony, which welcomes a new member into its circle. The single woman as witch is marginalized, excluded from the company, and when she complains in protest, this negative behavior is used as a further exoneration of the dominant social organization to legitimize her exclusion on the grounds of her inappropriate conduct. Representations of femininity in *Sleeping Beauty* are a good example for the nineteenth-century division of women into the elevated virtuous wife and mother, and the excluded negative side of femininity.[3] In this splitting into good and bad, the single woman, the working woman, and the relatively new feature of the publicly protesting woman are made to occupy the same position and are linked by association with the "traditional" incarnation of deviant femininity: the prostitute. Freeling, in fact, establishes an explicit link between a wife complaining about her husband's mistreatment of her and the immediate danger of her seduction, which was seen as the first, inevitable step toward prostitution (38–39). As a result, any role defined outside the radius of male influence is criminalized by association.

A good example for this is the case of Caroline Norton who lobbied for the right to her earnings and the right to keep her children after she had been forced to leave her husband because of his abusive behavior. She wrote two pamphlets in an attempt to influence public opinion and have the issue taken up by Parliament. Her first attempt, in 1837, *The Natural Claim of a Mother to the Custody of Her Child as Affected by Common Law Right of the Father* was unsuccessful, but her second pamphlet, *A Plain Letter* submitted under a male pseudonym, influenced the passing of the Infant Custody Bill in 1839. Although she was in every respect a good mother, nevertheless her actions excluded her from society, and she found herself in the ostracized position of an, in effect, "single" woman. Her case also presents another instance where an identifiable response to a particular historic moment of cultural crisis and anxiety can be traced in how the translations deal with the representation of femininity. In Taylor's 1839 text, the fairy is clearly identified as a single, bad woman who, like Norton, challenges authority with her "scolding" (27), disrupts the peace of the realm (palace) with her noise and interventions, and makes herself the subject of gossip. In fact, Norton was condemned for all of these (Moore 39–52).

By the end of the century, the evil-good dichotomy had been so firmly established that even Margaret Hunt's definitive translation, which was not aimed at the children's market but at restoring the Grimm collection to its status as a collection of scholarly source material, shows elements of emphasizing the differences between the good wise women and the bad one. However, Wehnert's 1853 text and its reprint had so far only hinted at her identity as a truly persecutory witch in 1857. As outlined earlier, the second strand of mytho-literary sources provided the motif configuration of sleep (as punishment)-male awakening presence (kiss)-persecution, and the motif of justified anger and punishment had been linked to the German tradition. The elements of persecution and jealousy play no role in the Grimm texts, but they are developed in the second half of Perrault's version where the prince's mother jealously persecutes her daughter-in-law. This plot development is displaced in later versions of the story onto the witch figure, who also amalgamates the old woman in the tower. As indicated above, this was only initiated by textual and paratextual developments in Wehnert's editions, which create a link between the evil fairy and the old woman in the tower, implying that her involvement in bringing about the fulfillment of the curse is not innocently accidental but the result of scheming. This was only fully developed in the twentieth century, when Disney's 1960 film fully established the demonization of the witch, whose curse on the princess is followed by her scheming plans to find her in the fifteen years when she is hidden by the good fairies in the forest. When the princess is brought to the palace on the last day that the curse can be realized, the witch lures the girl to her doom by manifesting as a green flame, thus hypnotizing her and leading her up into the little room. There the green flame turns into the spinning wheel and when the princess hesitates to touch the spindle, the witch's voice tells her to do so, just before the good fairies rush in. The witch assumes her own shape and gloatingly reveals her triumph over the princess, identifying herself as the mistress of all evil. Not only has she extended her malevolent influence into the little room, assuming both the spindle and the presence of the old woman for her persecution of the girl, but she also extends her efforts of keeping the princess from happiness by appropriating the hedge of thorns that becomes yet another impersonation of her evil force in the fight against the prince and the extended persecution of the princess.

Disney's film has played a crucial role in the understanding of this fairy tale and for many represents the definitive form of *Sleeping Beauty*. However, while Disney's version is a climax in the development from wise woman to evil witch, it also marks an end point to this process of construction. With deconstructive and feminist approaches to criticism, an increasing awareness of the constructedness of fairy tales and fairy tale characters has focused attention on the way gender roles are encoded into fairy tales in dogmatic ways. Increasing information on the processes of canon formation in the individual cultures and, perhaps even more so, in the international fairy tale corpus has foregrounded the mechanisms of selection, de-selection, editing, and adapting, which have shaped fairy tales over a considerable period of time. Access to oral precursors, alternative versions, and cultural variants of popular stories that do not conform to the dominant models of gender organization has allowed insights into fairy tales as a naturalized artifact. Thus, fairy tales, far from being a straitjacket that enforces restricted meanings, have increasingly been recognized as a genre which is, historically, defined by change and adaptation. This "proteanity" of the fairy tale has been critically analyzed by feminist critics and appropriated, or made use of, by writers and editors. Supported by the understanding that that which has been constructed, can also be de-constructed, the figure of the witch has been reclaimed and revalidated in much of feminist revisionary rewriting of fairy tales. In Angela Carter's *The Lady of the House of Love*, for example, the curse originates from male tradition and heritage; in Irmtraud Morgner's *Trobadora Beatriz* the princess figure herself asks to be put to sleep in order to awake in less patriarchal times, and in Sheri Tepper's *Beauty* the "evil" fairy turns out to be one of the few good characters in the novel, intent on saving both the princess and the world by her "curse." Stories such as these query the figure of the witch, introduce complexity into narrative motivation, and return the character to some of its original roundedness, or conflicted and ambiguous nature.[4]

Notes

1. See Bacchilega's excellent summary of the history of feminist criticism of the fairy tale (Introduction 8–10) and Zipes for reprints of classic examples of early work.
2. It should be noted, however, that this description relates primarily to a narrow core of popular stories such as *Cinderella, Sleeping Beauty, Snow White, Beauty and the Beast*, or *Bluebeard* and disregards the many other types of fairy tales in which such stereotypical representations are not prevalent. However, in the processes of canon formation, many of these "alternative" tales were either excluded from influential print collections or were adapted to fit the pattern described above. One outcome of the work of feminist scholars and writers has been that many more of these stories are now available for a wider readership. Nevertheless, the popular idea of the typical fairy tale still continues to be shaped by the passive-princess-male-savior paradigm.
3. The good fairies, however, also present a challenge to this dichotomy, calling into question the mutual exclusivity of the two categories of "The angel by the hearth" and "the fallen woman." Although they are unmarried, and thus single, textual logic requires that they have to be seen as "good." I believe that their representation as a community of twelve (i.e., not single), the emphasis on familial terms in describing them, such as sisterhood, and their integration into the nursery are an attempt to deal with this difficulty. Thus the emphasis on their caring, nurturing, and kindness to children codes them as good because they are seen to participate in the activities of motherhood.
4. For a more detailed discussion of the feminist revision of fairy tales and interpretation of Tepper's, Morgner's, and Carter's versions, see Karen Seago (2000) "Let Sleeping Beauties Lie? On the Difficulties of Revisioning the Tale." *New Comparison*, 27–8, pp. 1–20.

Works Cited

Bacchilega, Cristina. "An Introduction to the 'Innocent Persecuted Heroine' Fairy Tale." *Western Folklore* 52.1 (1993): 1–12.

———, ed. *Perspectives on the Innocent Persecuted Heroine in Fairy Tales.* Spec. issue of *Western Folklore* 52.1 (1993).

Bottigheimer, Ruth. *Grimms' Bad Girls & Bold Boys: The Moral & Social Vision of the Tales.* New Haven: Yale University Press, 1987.

Chapone, Mrs. *Letters on the Improvement of the Mind.* Edinburgh: Anderson, 1823.

Crane, Lucy, ed. and trans. *Household Stories.* By Jacob and Wilhelm Grimm. London: Macmillan & Co, 1882.

Davis, Matilda Louisa, ed. and trans. *Home Stories.* By Jacob and Wilhelm Grimm. London: Routledge and Co, 1855.

Duden, Barbara. "Das schöne Eigentum." *Kursbuch* 47 (1977): 125–40.

Freeling, Arthur. *The Young Bride's Book: Being Hints for Regulating the Conduct of Married Women. With a Few Medical Axioms.* London: Washbourne, 1839.

Gardiner, Alfonzo, ed. *Household Tales.* By Jacob and Wilhelm Grimm. Manchester: John Heywood, 1888.

[Gillies, Robert Pearse, ed. and trans.] *German Stories: Being Tales and Traditions Chiefly Selected from the Literature of Germany.* By Jacob and Wilhelm Grimm. Edinburgh: Fullerton & Co., 1855.

Grimm, Jacob. *Deutsche Mythologie.* Göttingen: Dieterich, 1835.

———. *Kleinere Schriften.* Vol. 8. Hildesheim: Georg Olms Verlagsbuchhandlung, 1965. Reprografischer Nachdruck der Ausgabe. Berlin, 1869.

———. *Teutonic Mythology: Supplement Collected from the Author's Post-Humous Notes.* Vol. 4. Prof. E. H. Meyer. Trans. J. S. Stallybrass. London: George Bell, 1900.

Grimm, Jacob, and Wilhelm Grimm. *Kinder- und Hausmärchen.* Vol 1. Berlin: Reimer, 1812.

———. *Kinder- und Hausmärchen.* Göttingen: Dieterich, 1850.

Held, Claudia. *Familienglück auf Bilderbogen. Die bürgerliche Familie des 19. Jahrhunderts im Spiegel der Neuruppiner Druckgraphik.* Bonn: Habelt, 1992.

Hunt, Margaret, ed. and trans. *Grimm's Household Tales.* By Jacob and Wilhelm Grimm. London: n. p., 1884.

Kamenetsky, Christa. *The Brothers Grimm and Their Critics: Folktales and the Quest for Meaning.* Athens: Ohio UP, 1992.

Matus, Jill. *Unstable Bodies, Victorian Representations of Sexuality and Maternity.* Manchester: Manchester UP, 1995.

Moore, Katharine. *Victorian Wives.* London: Allison & Busby, 1974.

Nelson, Claudia. "Sex and the Single Boy: Ideals of Manliness and Sexuality in Victorian Literature for Boys." *Victorian Studies* 32.4 (Summer 1989): 525–50.

Opie, Iona, and Peter Opie. *The Classic Fairy Tales.* New York: Paladin, 1974.

Palmegiano, E. M. *Women and British Periodicals*. New York: Garland, 1976.
Paull, Mrs. H. B., ed. and trans. *Grimms Fairy Tales*. By Jacob and Wilhelm Grimm. London: n. p., 1872.
Perrault, Charles. *Contes du temps passé de ma mère l'Oye, avec des morales*. 1697. London: van den Berg, 1764.
Poovey, Mary. *Uneven Developments, The Ideological Work of Gender in Mid-Victorian England*. London: Virago, 1988.
Rölleke, Heinz. "Nachwort." *Brüder Grimm Kinder-und Hausmärchen*. Ed. Heinz Stuttgart: Reclam, 1982. 590–617.
———. "Zur Biographie der Grimmschen Märchen." *Brüder Grimm, Kinder-und Hausmärchen*. Ed. Rölleke. Munich: Diederichs, 1989. 521–82.
Romain, Alfred. "Zur Gestalt des Grimmschen Dornröschen Märchens." *Zeitschrift für Volkskunde* 42 [new series 4] (1933):84–116.
Ruskin, John. Introduction. *German Popular Stories*. Ed. and trans. Edgar Taylor. London: Hotten, 1868. v-xiv.
[Samber, Robert, trans.]. *Histories, or Tales of Passed Times with Morals*. By Charles Perrault. 1729. 2nd ed. London: Montagu, Pote, 1737.
Schoof, Wilhelm. "Zur Geschichte des Grimmschen Märchenstils." *Der Deutschunterricht* 15.2 (June 1963): 90–99.
Seago, Karen. "Let Sleeping Beauties Lie? On the Difficulties of Revisioning the Tale." *New Comparison*, 27–8 (2000):1–20.
Seitz, Gabriele. *Die Brüder Grimm: Leben, Werk, Zeit*. München: Winkler, 1984.
Tatar, Maria. *Off with Their Heads! Fairy Tales and the Culture of Childhood*. Princeton: Princeton University Press, 1992. 15–19.
[Taylor, Edgar, ed. and trans.] *German Popular Stories*. By Jacob and Wilhelm Grimm. London: C. Baldwyn, 1823.
Taylor, Edgar, ed. and trans. *German Popular Stories and Fairy Tales as Told by Gammer Grethel*. By Jacob and Wilhelm Grimm. London: George Bell and Sons, 1839.
Walkowitz, Judith. *Prostitution and Victorian Society: Women, Class, and the State*. Cambridge: Cambridge University Press, 1982.
Wehnert, Edward, III. *Household Stories*. By Jacob and Wilhelm Grimm. London: Addey and Co, 1853.
Zipes, Jack. *Dont't Bet on the Prince*. Aldershot: Gower, 1986.

7

The Medieval Legend of the *Eaten Heart*

Ernesto Virgulti

During the Late Middle Ages in Europe, there circulated various versions of the macabre story of the *Eaten Heart*. It is essentially the tale of an adulterous love affair and of the ensuing vengeance of a betrayed husband. Although there are numerous variants, most versions of the story contain the following principal events. A romance develops between a man and the wife of another man; when the husband discovers his wife's adultery, he takes immediate steps not only to have her lover killed but also to have his heart cut out. The husband then has the heart made into a delectable meal, which he cunningly serves his unsuspecting wife at dinner. When it is revealed to her what she has eaten, the horrified wife dies or commits suicide.

In this chapter, I intend to trace the evolution of this story during its migration throughout Europe between the twelfth and fourteenth centuries. In so doing, I shall underscore and attempt to account for the similarities and differences found in the various versions of the *Eaten Heart* legend, then categorize these versions according to the interrelations of their narrative motifs. I use the term "motif" in a structuralist sense to designate a minimal narrative unit or a microsequence.[1] My intention is to focus on the more dominant motifs of the legend and to show how these motifs shift or migrate from one version to another. I shall point out that some motifs will remain constant in their migration, whereas others will inevitably change in form and meaning. As a literary sign, the motif's features will vary significantly from one work and cultural context to another.

In addition, I shall very briefly examine, from a narratological perspective, some of the structural components of the story and their relation to the components found in other tragic medieval tales belonging to the courtly love tradition. It is not my intention, however, to discuss cannibalism in general or examples of cannibalistic acts found in ancient mythology,[2] in folklore, or in the rites and rituals of various tribes and religions, including of course Christianity.[3] I am only concerned here with the eaten heart as a literary motif found within the context of the medieval tales of adultery or *fole amor*. As we shall see in the versions we are about to examine, it is the intention of the wronged husband to inflict the most cruel and barbaric punishment on his adulterous wife by forcing her to take part in the gruesome cannibalistic act of eating her lover's heart. However, for the wife, the heart of her lover holds a special significance not envisaged by the husband. As a result, the eating of the heart brings together both cannibalistic and erotic elements.

Some studies[4] indicate that the earliest known reference to the story of the *Eaten Heart* can be found in the twelfth century, in Thomas's version of the *Tristan and Iseult* legend.[5] In this work, there is an episode in which the sad Iseult sings a pitiful song of love, the *Lai Guiron,* which tells of the death of Guirun at the hands of a jealous and deceitful husband: "One day she sat in her chamber and made a sad lay of love—how my lord Guirun became enamored and was slain for love of the lady whom he cherished above all, and how thereupon, one day, in treachery the Count gave his wife Guirun's heart to eat, and what grief the lady felt when she learned of the death of her friend" (313). Unfortunately the lay of Guirun or Guiron is no longer extant. All that remains is a cursory reference, which makes it impossible to determine the date of composition, the author, or any of the details of the story.

The next reference to the eaten heart motif is contained in another lay, *Le Lai d'Ignaure ou Lai du Prisonnier,* written in the late twelfth or early thirteenth century by Renault de Beaujeu.[6] In this work, the protagonist, Ignaure, is a handsome and powerful knight, who is the lover of not one, but twelve women, all wives of barons. Discovering, by way of a mock confession, that they all have the same lover, the twelve infuriated ladies want to have Ignaure killed but then decide to spare him, provided he devote himself to only one of the women. However, the husband of the chosen lady soon learns of the relationship and has Ignaure put in prison. The ladies all protest and vow to maintain a fast until Ignaure is released. The twelve husbands deceive their wives by killing the lover, and with his heart and other parts of his body, they have twelve meals prepared, which are then given to their famished wives who have been fasting for days. When they discover the gruesome facts, the women vow never to eat again and subsequently die of starvation.

This rather extended version of the *Eaten Heart* legend (664 verses) introduces a number of variants, the major one being that of the multiple mistresses. This variant, in turn, has certain implications on the final meal of the twelve ladies. Although this rendition of the story is essentially tragic in structure, one cannot help but see an underlying element of parody in the "last supper" scene where the twelve women all share the body of Ignaure. However, the precise significance of the scene remains somewhat ambiguous. While the author's reenactment of the last supper can be viewed as parodic, it is not a comic parody. At the same time, I am doubtful that he was attempting to make a *figura Christi* out of the protagonist Ignaure, unless this, too, was intended as a parody. The allusion to the Christian rite of communion is clear as is his intent to integrate eucharistic and erotic elements in the story. The variants in this version and the subsequent *Novellino* tale are rather significant. For this reason, they should form a separate branch of the legend.

The Northern French *Lai d'Ignaure*, which introduces the variant of the multiple mistresses, is the source of the sixty-second story in the anonymous Italian work *Il Novellino*.[7] This very brief *novella* relates how the maids of a certain countess, wife of the feudal lord Roberto, take turns lying with the robust door-keeper, Bagliante. Hearing that Bagliante is of considerable proportions ("era a gran misura"), the countess herself decides to lie with him. When news of these escapades reaches Count Roberto, he has Bagliante killed and has a pie made of his heart, which he then serves the countess and her maids. The last part of the *novella,* however, does away with the traditional death motif of the mistresses. Aware of their loss of honor, the countess and her maids decide to become nuns and found a convent where they dedicate themselves to helping gentlemen travelers.

As we can see, many of the narrative motifs present in the *Novellino* tale derive from the *Lai d'Ignaure*, the major one being that of the multiple mistresses. The ending of the *Novellino* story differs in that it includes the motif of the nunnery, which seems to be an attempt on the part of the anonymous author to distinguish his version from the French *lay*. However, aside from this variant, the two accounts share a number of common traits which justifies placing them in a separate branch of the *Eaten Heart* legend. In fact, these versions can be read as parodies of the original tragic love story. The *Novellino* version, in particular, with its shift in structure from tragic to comic mode, goes well beyond the courtly love tradition. Indeed, it is the tale's hybridity, which fuses courtly elements and eucharistic imagery with the comic and erotic components found in the French *fabliau* genre,[8] that give the *Novellino* version not only a decidedly parodic or "carnivalesque" characteristic (in Mikhail Bakhtin's sense of the term)[9] but also a certain ambiguity of meaning and intent.

Chronologically, the next version of the legend is the *Vida* of *Guillem de Cabestaing,* but because it is the source of Boccaccio's fourteenth-century version, the two will be examined together in the subsequent sections. Two more courtly adaptations of the Eaten Heart legend are a lengthy French narrative poem titled *Le Roman du Châtelain de Couci* and a somewhat shorter German poem titled *Das Herze,* both late thirteenth-century works. In addition to considerably amplifying the original story, these versions contain a major shift in the narrative structure, namely the separation of the two lovers, which comes about as a result of the hero's departure. It is this motif that ultimately sets the following versions apart from all the others.

In the French poem, *Le Roman du Châtelain de Couci,* attributed to Jakemon Sakesep,[10] the hero, Renaut de Couci, a skillful knight and renowned poet, falls in love with La Dame de Faiel. He woos her through displays of gallantry (winning tournaments throughout the region) and by writing songs in her honor. In fact, more than one-half of the *Roman* deals with episodes related to Renaut's courtship of La Dame de Faiel. When the lady's husband discovers the adulterous relationship, rather than kill the lover, he devises a plan to rid himself of the gallant knight. The husband dupes Renaut into joining the Crusades in the Holy Land, where, after many acts of bravery, Renaut is mortally wounded. He attempts to return to France to see his lady, but his wounds prevent him from going beyond the southern Italian port of Brindisi. Before dying, Renaut commands his servant, Gobert, to cut out his heart, embalm it, and deliver it to his beloved, in a box together with a letter and the lady's braids, which she had given him upon departing. After Renaut's death, his servant carries out his wish. However, before the servant can see La Dame de Faiel, her husband intercepts the box containing the heart. He has the heart made into a savory meal, which is then served to his wife. When her husband reveals what she has just eaten, La Dame de Faiel is so horrified and devastatingly overwhelmed that she subsequently dies of grief.

Aside from a few minor variants, the narrative of the German poem, *Das Herze,*[11] written by Konrad von Würzburg, is based on the same motifs as the longer French work. Their similarity is due to the fact that they were written only a few years apart; more or less between 1284 and

1288. In the *Das Herze,* we have the traditional amorous relationship between a knight and a married woman. The knight must depart for the Holy Land, where he is so anguished that he dies of grief, not in battle. His squire executes the knight's dying wish, to cut out his heart and deliver it to his lady. The lady's husband confiscates the heart, which is in a golden box together with his wife's ring, then has his cook prepare a meal with the heart and serve it to his wife. When the husband reveals to his wife what she has eaten, she dies of such strong grief that her own heart bursts.

As we can see, these two works, which contain the major variant (first introduced in the *Roman*) of the lover's departure for the Crusades, form another distinct branch of *the Eaten Heart* legend. The motif can be attributed to the fact that a Châtelain de Coucy actually did take part in and die during the Third Crusade to the Holy Land (1189–92), but his name was Gui de Thourotte,[12] not Renaut. Moreover, there is no historical record of the heart incident ever having taken place. Renaut is, however, the name of the author of the previously examined *Lai d'Ignaure*. These facts serve to illustrate that not only these versions, but stories in general, stem from and develop out of a composite of literary motifs and real-life sources.

From a narratological perspective, the motif of the lover's departure, introduced in the *Roman,* signals a shift that inevitably alters the traditional story structure. Distanced from the other characters, the death of the lover comes about, not at the hands of the jealous husband but as a result of a mortal wounding in battle. The lover's final request that his servant extract his heart and deliver it to his beloved not only functions as proof of the knight's everlasting fidelity to his lady, but it is above all an indispensable narrative component that serves to link up the story's final sequence of motifs (the husband's treachery, the consuming of the heart, and the death of the lady). In some way, the lover's heart must reach the beloved, and the story must reach its inevitable, tragic conclusion.

A much later popular British version of 1707[13] is structurally identical to the two versions just examined, but it contains some amusing cultural twists on the semantic level. In this English rendition, the lover, mortally wounded in battle, has his servant cut out his heart and bake it to a powder. It is then sent to his lady back in England. The semantic variant of the heart baked to a powder inevitably generates another variant. The suspecting husband intercepts the powdered heart, then devises a uniquely British way to get his wife to ingest the powdered heart—he puts it in her tea! This rather amusing example demonstrates how storytelling motifs are clearly subject to and indeed determined by historical and cultural factors that influence both the production and the reception of stories.

The three versions just examined (*Le Roman du Châtelain de Couci, Das Herze*, and the anonymous British tale) contain variants that serve to illustrate how motifs shift in their migration from one version to another. The death of the lover, for example, is a constant and structurally unavoidable motif in all the *Eaten Heart* tales. However, exactly how the lover dies depends on the other motifs comprising the narrative structure of each story. If the lover departs, he cannot be killed by the husband but has to die by some other means. Whether he is slain by the jealous husband or mortally wounded in battle is determined by other motifs introduced into the story (in this case, the lover's departure). Similarly, the extracted heart, in the three versions just examined, is either embalmed or baked to a powder on account of the great distance separating the two lovers, once again as the result of the hero's departure. Motifs are clearly interrelated, and the introduction of any variant, such as the departure of the lover, will in turn trigger other changes in the story.

The last two versions to be examined, a Provençal *vida* and one of Boccaccio's *novellas* (*December* IV, 9), were written more than a century apart. However, they do share some characteristics. The first is the *Vida,* or Biography, of the *Troubadour Guillem de Cabestaing*. In fact, there are four, somewhat incomplete versions.[14] In this early thirteenth-century Provençal *Vida,* Guillem de Cabestaing, troubadour and vassal of Raimond de Rossillon, falls in love with and begins to woo his lord's wife, Saurimonda. Raimond's jealousy is aroused upon hearing one of Cabestaing's love songs. Thus, he arranges to meet the troubadour away from the castle, where he kills him, tears out his heart, and, in three versions, decapitates him. Raimond subsequently has the heart roasted and served to his wife. Afterwards, he tells her what she has eaten and, as proof, shows her Cabestaing's head. Raimond then pursues her with his sword, but she runs to the balcony and jumps to her death. The epilogue of the *Vida* contains further innovations in that the husband is punished by none other than King Alphonse of Aragon himself. It is the king who confiscates Raimond's lands, destroys his castles, and puts him in prison where he perishes. The two lovers, on the other hand, are buried in the same tomb, which is placed in front of the church in Perpignan, where the knights and ladies of the entire county come annually to commemorate the anniversary of their death.

With this rather hyperbolized epilogue, the author of the *Vida* intends to glorify the sufferings of the two protagonists and condemn those, like the husband, who would stand in the way of true love. Although the *Vida* claims to be biographical, it must be pointed out that, once again, the author(s) incorporated a combination of fact and fiction in formulating the account(s). First, King Alphonse of Aragon could not have punished Raimond because he died in 1196, a year before the marriage of Raimond and his wife Saurimonda. Second, not only did the real Saurimonda not die on account of her lover, she went on to marry another man, Adhemar de Mosset, ten years after her marriage to Raimond. This Provençal *Vida* does, however, contain some important motifs, such as the ambush and murder of the lover by the husband himself and his subsequent punishment, which Boccaccio assimilates into his adaptation of the tale.

The structural components of Boccaccio's version (*Decameron* IV, 9) are analogous to the *Vida* of the Troubadour. In fact, in the introduction to his story, the ninth *novella* of the fourth day of the *Decameron,* Boccaccio acknowledges that his source comes from Provence.[15] However, Boccaccio's *novella* contains features that add a dimension of literariness to his work. It is the tale of two knights named Guiglielmo Guardastagno and Guiglielmo Rossiglione, who share a strong and intimate friendship. They are of equal rank and are equally skilled as knights. They attend jousting tournaments together and even wear identical attire: " . . . both men excelled in feats of daring, they were bosom friends and made a point of accompanying one another to jousts and tournaments and other armed contests, each bearing the same device" (388).

Boccaccio not only takes great care in underscoring the closeness and sameness of the two knights, he even gives them the same first name, Guiglielmo. Moreover, to further reinforce the focus on the intimate relationship of the two Guiglielmos, the author does not give a name to Rossiglione's wife. By emphasizing the motif of friendship and brotherhood, the author lays the groundwork for the eventual severing of these bonds. Thus, Boccaccio establishes, from the outset, a motivation for the actions of his characters not present in the Provençal *Vida,* for example. Boccaccio's two knights have so much in common that it is almost inevitable for them to love the same woman and for the same woman to be attracted to both men.

Moreover, when Rossiglione is later betrayed by his wife and best friend, the adulterous act carries with it a heightened sense of transgression, for it is at once a violation of marriage and a violation of friendship. This double deception, in turn, justifies the savagery of the betrayed Rossiglione's revenge, at least in his eyes. It is significant that when Rossiglione discovers the adultery, his initial reaction is one of rage, not toward his wife but toward his best friend Guardastagno. In fact, he "was so incensed . . . that his great love for Guardastagno was transformed into mortal hatred" (389).

Rossiglione then plots his revenge. In a nearby forest, he ambushes Guardastagno, who is unarmed. In a fit of rage, he drives a lance through his friend's breast, screaming: "Traitor, you are dead!" (389). Rossiglione's insatiable thirst for vengeance then drives him to take a knife, cut open his friend's chest, and extract his heart. The heart is brought back to his castle, where he orders his cook to prepare the most succulent dish possible with it, telling him it is the heart of a boar. The cook, "employing all his skill and loving care," turned it into "a dish that was too exquisite for words" (390). That evening the delectable yet gruesome meal is brought to the table in a silver tureen for Rossiglione's wife to eat. The betrayed husband's atrocious punishment of the two lovers is complete.

Upon discovering what she has eaten, Lady Rossiglione lashes out at her husband in a scathing condemnation of his actions. Determined that no other food shall ever pass her lips, after having partaken of such a "noble meal,"[16] Lady Rossiglione rushes to a nearby window and jumps to her death. She not only dies, but is "almost completely disfigured" by the fall (391). Overcome by remorse, shocked by the horrible spectacle, and fearing the castigation of the people and the Count of Provence, Rossiglione flees. Intending to punish and forever separate the two lovers, Rossiglione unwittingly unites them in death. The following day, the people of the district gather the remains of the two lovers and bury them in a single tomb.

The versions examined so far can be schematized into the following three categories:

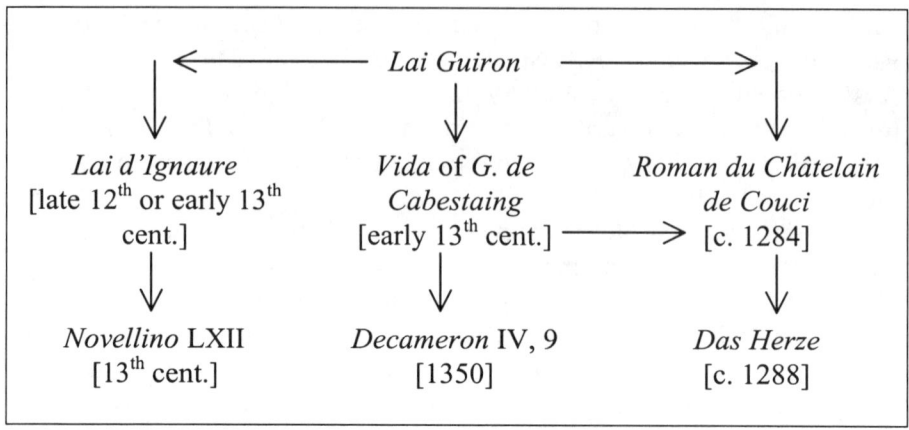

Figure 1. Versions of the *Eaten Heart* Legend

Figure 1, based on what is known about the legend, is an attempt on my part to illustrate the evolution and migration of the legend and to underline the interrelations of the various versions, all of which, I propose, have as a source the *Lai Guiron*. It is conceivable, however, that the preceding tales have as their source a version other than the *Lai Guiron* that no longer exists. Likewise, it is possible that the *Roman du Châtelain de Couci* derives from the *Vida of Guilhem de Cabestaing* (hence the arrow connecting the two) because, like the *Roman*, the *Vida* amplifies the enamourment of the two protagonists and contains embedded poems.

Let us now briefly examine some of the structural components of these stories and their relation to other tragic medieval tales. I shall focus on Boccaccio's *novella* because the motifs in this account show that he was well aware of the structure of *Romance* and the narrative components of the *contes d'adultères* or *fole amor*. Moreover, Boccaccio's version is the most literary in its portrayal, development, and motivation of the characters.

Boccaccio's *novella* is more than a simple tale of adultery; it is also a story of the betrayal of an intimate friendship. By introducing the motif of brotherhood or common bond that links the lover to the husband, Boccaccio sets the stage for the eventual severing of these bonds through the act of adultery. This motif can be found in other well-known romances. In the story of *Lancelot and Guinevere,* for example, Lancelot is linked to King Arthur through vassalage. Similarly, in the romance of

Tristan and Iseult, Tristan is both vassal and nephew of Iseult's husband, King Mark. The same motif can be found in Dante's *Divine Comedy.* In the fifth Canto of the *Inferno,* Dante introduces us to two lovers, Paolo and Francesca, who were killed by Francesca's husband, Gianciotto. Here, the adultery of Paolo and Francesca is an even more serious violation because Paolo's betrayal is against his own brother, Gianciotto. For this reason, Dante condemns the two lovers (in-laws) to Hell. It follows, therefore, that the closer the bonds linking the characters together, the more serious and injurious the transgression of the adulterers, and the more fervent the ensuing vengeance on the part of the deceived husband. Thus, the savagery of Rossiglione's revenge certainly becomes justified from a structural and motivational point of view (albeit not from a moral perspective), when, and only when, the bonds of brotherhood that link the two Guiglielmos are broken. Moreover, it is only in the context of Boccaccio's *novella* that we can begin to understand the motivation behind the tearing out of the heart. In the other versions, the husband's sadistic actions lack justification and real motivation.

The second motif under consideration is that of the lady's suicide. This motif is virtually inevitable in tragic love stories of this type. Deprived of her lover, without whom she cannot live, the lady must now follow him in death. Thus, the lady's suicide becomes, at once, an act of fidelity toward her lover and an act of denial toward her husband, who has put an end to their romance. In the versions of the *Vida* and of the *Decameron,* the variant of a brutally violent suicide is introduced. Boccaccio further develops this variant, thereby adding structural continuity and symmetry to his narrative. Just as her lover's body is savagely dismembered by her husband, so, too, is Lady Rossiglione's body severely mutilated and "almost completely disfigured" (391) in plummeting to her death.

Deprived of the fulfillment of their passion in life, the two lovers are finally united in death as they are buried in a single tomb, another motif found in such tragic love stories as that of *Tristan and Iseult* and Ovid's *Pyramus and Thisbe.* In this latter story two young lovers, whose parents oppose their marriage, plan to meet outside the city in order to run away together. Pyramus, finding a blood-stained veil and thinking his beloved Thisbe has been killed, has no choice but to commit suicide. When Thisbe discovers his body, she takes Pyramus's sword and follows him in death. The parents are overcome by the tragedy. As a result, "the remains of the two lovers, gathered from the funeral fires, rest together in a single urn" (Ovid 98).

The motif of the lady's suicide as well as that of the lovers united in death appear in another of Boccaccio's *novellas*, the first story of Day IV. In this *novella,* Ghismonda, the daughter of Tancredi, Prince of Salerno, refuses to put an end to the affair with her father's valet, Guiscardo. The father has Guiscardo killed and sends his daughter the heart of her lover in a golden chalice. Upon realizing what her father has sent her, Ghismonda prepares a poisonous potion, pours it into the chalice containing the heart, and then drinks it. Afterwards, lying on her bed, she takes Guiscardo's heart, places it next to hers, and waits for the lethal potion to take effect. Realizing what he has done and overcome with grief and remorse, Tancredi, has the two lovers buried honorably together in a single tomb.[17]

In closing, let us turn to the heart itself, which lies at the very core of the narrative. The heart is the object toward which the three main characters of the story are drawn and to which they manifest either their passionate love or their violent, vengeful hatred. For the betrayed husband, the tearing out of the lover's heart is a manifestation of his vehement, latent desire to castrate his rival and to punish his wife in a truly sadistic manner. Clearly, it is the husband's intention to inflict the most atrocious punishment possible on the two adulterers. For this reason, the lover is disemboweled, and the errant wife is forced to partake of the macabre meal. However, the husband is unaware of the heart's other significance. By deceitfully compelling his wife to eat the heart as retribution, the husband unknowingly joins together the two lovers whom he intended to divide. The husband's final act of vengeance turns out to be the ultimate assertion and confirmation of love. Symbolically, in both his stories, Boccaccio frames the heart in eucharistic imagery: Guardastagno's heart is brought to Lady Rossiglione in a silver tureen (*Decameron* IV, 9), and Guiscardo's heart is brought to his beloved Ghismonda in a golden chalice (*Decameron* IV, 1). Unlike the other versions of the legend, the eating of the heart in Boccaccio's novella is not intended as a mere literal representation. He transforms the consuming of the heart into a metaphor for the physical and spiritual union—or "communion"—of the two lovers. In Boccaccio's text, the heart becomes, at once, the symbolic representation of the union of the lovers and noble food that will nourish and sustain their passion forever.

Notes

1. Among the first to use the term motif in this context were the Russian Formalists, in particular Boris Tomashevsky, for whom the term signified a nucleus of narrative or an irreducible semantic unit (see Tomashevsky's "Thematics" in *Russian Formalist Criticism*). Naturally, other formalists like Vladimir Propp developed similar theories in an attempt to classify recurring story elements. Propp formulated a theory based on *functions* (see *The Morphology of the Folktale*), while the structuralists and narratologists who followed Propp (Barthes, Todorov, Genette, Chatman, and so forth) elaborated similar theories in their attempts to isolate structural elements in narrative (see Roland Barthes's "Introduction à l'analyse structurale des récits" in the legendary volume of *Communications* 8, 1966, pp. 1–27. This volume contains some of the first structuralist theories of Barthes, Bremond, Genette, Greimas, and Todorov). Finally, folklorists have used, and continue to use, the notion of motif in a broad, thematic sense as a means of classifying major aspects of folktales (see Stith Thompson, *Motif-Index of Folk-Literature*). I wish to point out that one of the pioneers in the area of motifs and folktales was Alexander Veselovsky (1838–1906), who influenced the work of the Formalists (see L. T. Lemon and M. J. Reis's "Introduction" in *Russian Formalist Criticism: Four Essays*).
2. One example in ancient mythology of the heart motif linked to the act of cannibalism can be found in a version of the Dionysus myth in which Zeus's favorite son, Dionysus, was torn to pieces by the Titans. Athena saved his heart, which was then given to Zeus to eat. From Zeus's union with the Princess Semele, and the heart serving as the seed, Dionysus was reborn. Hence the name Dionysus which signifies "twice-born god." For more on this myth, see Meyer Reinhold, *Past and Present: The Continuity of Classical Myths*.
3. The practice of entering into communion with a deity by the eating of his or her effigy in order to acquire some of the god's power or virtue seems to be a particularly widespread custom. In many religions, this rite was—and still is today—carried out symbolically, as in the Christian rite of Communion, whereas some ancient tribes like the Pueblo Indians exercised the rite in a literal manner. On the Pueblo Indians, see L. H. Gray, *The Mythology of All Races,* vol. x (202–4).
4. Most of the studies dealing with the *Eaten Heart* legend appeared between the end of the nineteenth century and the beginning of the twentieth. The focus of these studies was on sources and analogues and not on literary or structural analysis. The first to draw our attention to these tales was Gaston Paris with two studies (essentially the same): "Le Roman du Châtelain de Couci" in *Romania* VIII (1879): 343–73, and "Jakemon Sakesep, Auteur du Roman du Châtelain du Couci" in *Histoire Littéraire de la France*, vol. 28 (1881): 352–90. Subsequently, John E. Matzke published two similar studies: "The Legend of the Eaten Heart" in *Modern Language Notes* 26 (1911): 1–8, and "The *Roman du Châtelain de Couci* and Fauchet's

Chronique" in *Studies in Honour of A. Marshall Elliott*, vol. 1 (1911): 1–18. See also Henri Hauvette "La 39e Nouvelle du *Décaméron* et la Légend du 'Coeur Mangé'" in *Études sur Boccacce* [1894–1916] (1968): 184–205.

5. References to the surviving fragments of the *Tristan* version of Thomas can be found in the *Tristan* edition of Gottfried Von Strassburg, trans. A. T. Hatto (1967).
6. All references to this work are taken from Renaut [de Beaujeau]*Le Lai d'Ignaure ou Lai du Prisonnier*, Ed. Rita Lejeune (Bruxelles: Academie Royale de Langue et de Littératures Françaises de Belgique, 1938).
7. The novella of *Messer Ruberto*, number LXII, can be found in Sebastiano Lo Nigro's edition *Novellino e Conti del Duecento* (Torino: UTET, 1964): 153–55.
8. The fabliaux were comic narrative poems (normally 300–400 lines in length) of a bawdy or satirical nature. The genre prevailed in France between the late twelfth and fourteenth centuries.
9. In his *Rabelais and His World*, Bakhtin develops the notion of the "carnival" element in literature, which is essentially a parodic and satirical mode of writing. It is subversive in that it challenges literary traditions and the official culture of the time.
10. See Gaston Paris: "Jakemon Sakesep, Auteur du Roman du Châtelain de Couci." In his study, "The Legend of the Eaten Heart" in *Modern Language Notes* 26 (1911):1–8, John E. Matzke attributes the *Roman* to Jakemes Makes, while in his second study he suggests that Jakemon Maket should be accepted as the author's correct name. See "The *Roman du Châtelain de Couci* and Fauchet's *Chronique*" in *Studies in Honour of A. Marshall Elliott*, vol. 1 (Baltimore: Johns Hopkins University Press, 1911): 1–18.
11. My brief summary of the *Das Herze* is based on the English account found in Matzke's aforementioned study, "The *Roman du Châtelain de Couci* and Fauchet's *Chronique*," 16–17.
12. See Maurice Delbouille's Introduction to *Le Roman du Châtelain de Couci* (by Jakemes 1285; Paris: Société des Anciens Textes Français, (1936); in particular, pages XLVI–XLVIII.
13. This British version of the *Eaten Heart* legend, of unknown authorship, is found in W. A. Clouston,'s *Popular Tales and Fictions: Their Migrations and Transformations*, 191. Belonging to the oral tradition, the tale has no formal title. It is simply known as the story of "The Constant but Unhappy Lovers."
14. For the various versions of the *Vida* of *Guillem De Cabestaing,* see Arthur Langfors "Le Troubadour Guilhem de Cabestanh," in *Annales du Midi* 26 (1914); Jean Boutière and A. H. Schutz, *Biographies des Troubadours: Textes Provençaux des XIIIe et XIVe Siècles* (New York: Burt Franklin, 1950): 154–72; *Le biografie trovadoriche: testi provenzali dei sec. XIII e XIV,* ed. Guido Favati (Bologna: Libreria Antiquaria Palmaverde,1961): 197–208; and *The Vidas of the Troubadours,* trans. Margarita Egan (New York & London: Garland Publishing, 1984): 53–55. Regrettably, M. Egan's edition has many omissions and contains only two versions of the *Vida of G. de Cabestanh.*

15. In the introduction to the tale, Boccaccio states: "You must know, then, that according to the Provençals, there lived in Provence two noble knights, each of whom owned several castles . . ." (*The Decameron* 388). In order to remain as faithful as possible to the original Italian text, I am using the names which Boccaccio employs, Guiglielmo Rossiglione and Guiglielmo Guardastagno, not the French adaptation of the names chosen by the English translator, McWilliam, Guillaume de Roussillon and Guillaume de Cabestanh. Further references to Boccaccio's *novella* are taken from this edition and will appear in the text.
16. I use the phrase "noble meal" to refer to the repast made from Guardastagno's heart because Boccaccio's original Italian text states: "nobil vivanda." Unfortunately, McWilliam translates the phrase as "such excellent fare," which does not convey the same idea. The words are those of Lady Rossiglione, and to her, clearly, this is a noble and sublime meal.
17. For some insightful observations on Boccaccio's *novella* of Ghismonda and Tancredi (*Dec*. IV, 1), see Giuseppe Mazzotta's chapter "The Heart of Love" (*The World at Play in Boccaccio's Decameron*).

Works Cited

Alighieri, Dante. *The Divine Comedy 1. Inferno.* Trans. Dorothy L. Sayers. Middlesex, England: Penguin Books, 1955.
Bakhtin, Mikhail. *Rabelais and His World.* Trans. Helene Iswolsky. Cambridge: Massachusetts Institute of Technology, 1968.
Barthes, Roland. "Introduction à l'analyse structurale des récits." *Communications* 8 (1966): 1–27.
Boccaccio, Giovanni. *The Decameron.* Trans. G. H. McWilliam. Middlesex, England: Penguin Books, 1972.
Boutière, Jean, and A.H. Schutz. *Biographies des Troubadours: Textes Provençaux des XIIIe et XIVe Siècles.* New York: Burt Franklin, 1950.
Clouston, W. A. *Popular Tales and Fictions: Their Migrations and Transformations.* Vol. 2. Edinburg & London: W. Blackwood and Sons, 1887.
Delbouille, Maurice and John E. Matzke, eds. *Le Roman du Châtelain de Couci.* By Jakemes. 1285. Paris: Société des Anciens Textes Français, 1936.
Egan, Margarita, trans. *The Vidas of the Troubadours.* New York: Garland Publishing, 1984.
Favati, Guido. Ed. *Le* biografie *trovadoriche: testi provenzali dei sec. XIII e XIV.* Bologna: Libreria Antiquaria Palmaverde, 1961.
Gray, Louis H, ed. *The Mythology of All Races.* Vol. X. New York: Cooper Square Publishers, 1964.
Hauvette, Henri. "La 39e Nouvelle du Décaméron et la Legend du Coeur Mangé." *Études sur Boccacce* [1894–1916]. Torino: Bottega d'Erasmo, 1968. 184–205.
Langfors, Arthur. "Le Troubadour Guilhem de Cabestanh." *Annales du Midi* 26 (1914).
Lo Nigro, Sebastiano, ed. *Novellino e Conti del Duecento.* Torino: UTET, 1964.
Matzke, John E. "The Legend of the Eaten Heart." *Modern Language Notes* 26 (1911): 1–8.
———. "The *Roman du Châtelain de Couci* and Fauchet's *Chronique.*" *Studies in Honour of A. Marshall Elliot.* Vol. 1. Baltimore: Johns Hopkins University Press, 1911. 1–18.
Mazzotta, Giuseppe. *The World at Play in Boccaccio's Decameron.* Princeton: Princeton University Press, 1986.
Ovid. *Metamorphoses.* Trans. Mary M. Innes. Middlesex: Penguin Books, 1973.
Paris, Gaston. "Jakemon Sakesep, Auteur du Roman du Châtelain du Couci." *Histoire Littéraire de la France.* Vol. 28 (1881): 352–390.
———. "Le Roman du Châtelain de Couci." *Romania* 8 (1879): 343–73.
Propp, Vladimir. *Morphology of the Folktale.* Trans. Laurence Scott. Texas: University of Texas Press, 1968.
Reinhold, Meyer. *Past and Present: The Continuity of Classical Myths.* Toronto: Hakkert, 1972.
Renaut [de Beaujeau]. *Le Lai d'Ignaure ou Lai du Prisonnier.* Ed. Rita Lejeune. Bruxelles: Academie Royale de Langue et de Littératures Françaises de Belgique, 1938.

Thompson, Stith. *Motif-Index of Folk-Literature*. Rev. ed. Bloomington: Indiana University Press, 1955.
Tomashevsky, Boris. "Thematics." *Russian Formalist Criticism: Four Essays*. Ed. and trans. L. T. Lemon, and M. J. Reis. Lincoln: University of Nebraska Press, 1965. 59–95.
Von Strassburg, Gottfried. *Tristan, With the Tristan of Thomas*. Trans. A. T. Hatto. Middlesex: Penguin Books, 1967.

8

The *Geist* of the Grimms

Allyson Wenzowski and Debi Keir-Nicholson

The dreamer awakes, The shadow goes by; When I tell you a tale, The tale is a lie. But ponder it well, Fair maiden, good youth: The tale is a lie, What it tells is the truth.

—Alice, Kane, *The Dreamer Awakes*

From 6 September to 25 October 1998, the McMaster Museum of Art mounted an exhibition of twentieth-century German art, with an emphasis on major Expressionist artists and other artists key to this important art movement.[1] The exhibition entitled *Geist*, translated from the German as "spirit, intellect or mind" (Wiginton), illustrated the philosophy of Expressionism, wherein inner nature took precedence over outer, descriptive representation. The Expressionist artist used elements of the outer visual world to convey an interior vision while distorting the elements depicted in the interests of a more powerful expressiveness. In 1912 the German intellectual Carl Einstein stated in the journal *Die Aktion* that, "... the role of art was to achieve a liberation from everything that everyday reality imposed ... and to accomplish, thanks to individual creative and imaginary impulses, a reconstruction" (Richard 9–10).

As a follow-up to *Geist*, in March of 1999, Dundas Storyspinners held a storytelling concert at the McMaster Museum of Art. The storytelling concert was called *The "Geist" of Grimms,* and the stories were told in conjunction with the display of four works from McMaster's *Geist* exhibition: Edvard Munch's woodcut, *The Kiss*, 1902 (Figure 1), Ernst Barlach's cast bronze, *The Transition*, 1917 (Figure 2), Emil Nolde's woodcut, *Marching Warriors*, 1917 (Figure 3), and Otto Dix's two color lithograph, *Leonie,* 1923 (Figure 4).

Figure 1. Edvard Munch, *Der Kuss / The Kiss*, 1902.

Two-color woodblock, black and grey, on tissue-thin Japan paper.
Credits: Christie's, London, England (via agent). Levy Bequest Purchase.
McMaster University Collection, Hamilton, Canada. Photo: Isaac Applebaum.
Reprinted by permission.

Figure 2. Ernst Barlach, *Der Übergang / The Transition*, 1917.

Cast bronze relief, 3/3.
Credits: Karl und Faber, Munch (via agent). Levy Bequest Purchase. McMaster
University Collection, Hamilton, Canada. Photo: Isaac Applebaum. Reprinted
by permission.

Figure 3. Emil Nolde, *Ziehende Krieger / Marching Warriors*, 1917.
Woodcut.
Credits: Nolde-Stiftung Seebüll. Anonymous Gift; Das Kunsthaus, Mannheim. McMaster University Collection, Hamilton, Canada. Photo: Courtesy McMaster Museum of Art. Reprinted by permission.

Figure 4. Otto Dix, *Leonie*, 1923.
Two-color, green and rose, lithograph
Credits: Estate of Otto Dix/VG Bild-Kunst (Bonn)/SODRAC (Montreal) 2000. Villa Grisebach, Berlin (via Agent). Levy Bequest Purchase. McMaster University Collection, Hamilton, Canada. Photo: Isaac Applebaum.
Reprinted by permission.

The tales told by Dundas Storyspinners were the Grimms' *Aschenputtel*[2] (Cinderella), *Mother Hulde*[3] (or Mother Holle*)*, *Cat and The Mouse in Partnership*,[4] *The Queen Bee*,[5] *The Turnip*,[6] *The Woodcutter's Child*[7] (or *Our Lady's Child*), and Kay Stone's *The Curious Girl*,[8] based on the Grimms' *Mother Trude*[9] (*Frau Trude*). The concert was held in the Education Centre of the Museum. The event was advertised both on and off campus. The event was well attended, photographs were taken, and a follow-up article appeared in the local paper, the *Dundas Star News*.

The juxtaposition of early twentieth-century German Expressionist art with tales from the Brothers Grimm of a century earlier demonstrates striking commonalities between the art and the stories. Both the stories and the art deal with the overarching motif of the spiritual quest in the Western European tradition which encompasses the themes of life and death, good and evil, redemption and transformation, and the important underlying belief that the outer landscape (external reality) is a reflection of the inner landscape (interior subjectivity), with the inner landscape having priority. Issues of isolation, sublimation, linearity, simplification, and abstraction of design are also common to both Expressionist art and the Grimms' tales. In both, the exaggeration and simplification of color and form remain central to the invocation of a strong emotional response on the part of the viewer or listener.

Origins of German Expressionism

The Expressionist art movement in Germany started with Dresden's artist group, The *Brücke* (Bridge) founded in 1905 and Munich's *Blauer Reiter*, founded in 1911 (Rosenberg 301). Child art, folk art, and primitive art appealed to German Expressionists because of the simplicity and raw emotional power of these art forms, and Early German woodcuts of the fifteenth century provided a key inspiration for the movement. Thus, the graphic art of the woodcut became a key player in German Expressionism, and the rugged and dynamic qualities of the woodcut technique with its clear lines and bold shapes provided artists with a means to communicate the strength of their feelings through a powerful and emotionally charged method of execution and intentional expressive distortion of form (301–2).

Other graphic media, especially drypoint and lithography, appealed to the Expressionist artist because of their ability to convey the artist's interior vision quickly and directly. Subjects depicted included land and city scapes, searing psychological portraits and social and religious themes revealing a deep concern for the problems of modern life and a spiritual longing. In the words of the artist Oskar Kokoschka, "Let us understand Expressionism as the living voice of man, who is to recreate his universe . . ." (Greenwood 2).

Intimacy

Edvard Munch's *The Kiss* and the Grimms' *Cat and Mouse in Partnership* both reveal part of "the living voice of man [and woman]" in the sphere of human relationships. Munch's image shows a couple embracing. They are as one; the smaller (female) figure appears to be submerged in, or perhaps dominated by, the larger (male) figure. There is very little modeling; a few carved lines render the figures that appear as a flattened silhouette in the extreme foreground. The background is virtually nonexistent: a grey toned backdrop. These two joined figures exist as one in isolation, further emphasizing the dominance of the larger male figure bending down, surrounding, perhaps devouring, the smaller female. The image is ambivalent; the darkness of the forms and their intermingling hint at the potential malevolent aspect of the relationship between two lovers.

There is no mistake in the nature of the relationship between the characters in the Grimms' *Cat and Mouse in Partnership*. In the opening line we are told that, "A cat having made acquaintance with a mouse, professed such great love . . . that the mouse at last agreed that they should keep house together" (Junior Deluxe ed. 47). As with all traditional Western European fairy tales, we are given no background information about the two characters: the town they live in, their families, and so forth. Similarly to the two figures in *The Kiss,* the cat and the mouse exist in isolation on a flat background.

The cat quickly shows his domination of the little mouse, subtly and slyly using mind games: " . . . You little mouse must not stir out, or you will be caught in a trap" (47). The cat and the mouse sanctify and solidify their relationship. They take counsel together and buy a pot of fat which they store in the church and which they promise not to touch until the winter. However, the cat soon breaks his vow, and when the little mouse voices her suspicions, the cat sneeringly says, "That's because you are always sitting at home . . . in your little grey frock and hairy tail, never seeing the world, and fancying all sorts of things" (50). Later, when the mouse confronts the cat with the proof of his infidelity, the cat screams, "Will you hold your tongue . . . another word, and I devour you too!" (51). The mouse's accusation, though, cannot be taken back, and so we are told that "the cat leaped upon her and made an end of her. And that is the way of the world" (51). Unfortunately, that was, and still is, the way of an unlucky number of intimate relationships. Thus, the control, domination, and violence that are hinted at in *The Kiss* become actualized in as *Cat and Mouse in Partnership*. *Cat and Mouse in Partnership* thus acts an allegory of male/female violence, whereas *The Kiss* contains, in the simplicity of its graphic image, the seed for the corrosive behavior that may come.

Eros and Duality

Munch's woodcut, *The Kiss*, as a symbol of sexual passion, also encompasses the tender aspects of eros. The two figures are blending into each other; as lovers, they wish to be together, to belong together, to become one. This exclusivity on the part of lovers is seen in the Grimms' *Aschenputtel*. When the prince first meets Aschenputtel he immediately falls in love, ". . . and [he] took her by the hand and danced with her, and he refused to stand up with any one else, so that he might not be obliged to let go her hand; and when any one came to claim it he answered, 'She is my partner'" (138).

The prince is so possessed by Aschenputtel that he follows her home. On the third night, desperate to discover her whereabouts, he manages, through subterfuge, to keep her left slipper which, as we know, is crucial to the final joining of the prince and Aschenputtel. Instantly, when the golden slipper is put on her little foot, ". . . the prince looked in her face, [and] he knew again the beautiful maiden that had danced with him, and he cried, 'this is the right bride!'" (138). The prince is in a hurry to find a bride, and Aschenputtel makes no effort to delay the nuptials. This is the way with fairy tales; true love comes quickly and the wedding is fast. *Aschenputtel* can thus be seen as a metaphor for the eros depicted in *The Kiss*. The fitting of a golden slipper onto a delicate little foot sublimates the eroticism of the Edvard Munch image.

The Kiss is intriguing in yet another aspect as it depicts the Western concept of duality: the duality of the sexes, and thus the duality of life, the duality of good and evil, of black and white, of night and day. *The Kiss* both shows and contemplates the momentary stillness that occurs when forces are in balance and at a point of peace. It is a moment of complete and utter stillness, of perfect accord and happiness, the calm before the storm. So, too, the cat and mouse are in balance and are still when they first decide to be together. However, things cannot remain as they are; movement and conflict are needed for change and growth, whether it be Aschenputtel's dance with the prince or the cat's treachery to the mouse.

Change and Transformation

Ernst Barlach was an accomplished sculptor, printmaker, illustrator, and writer, and by 1925 he was regarded as one of Germany's leading sculptors (Ness 52). *The Transition*, a cast bronze relief from 1917, had its beginnings in a trip that Barlach took in 1906 to visit his brother in Russia (52). This trip greatly affected the future direction of Barlach's work. The simplicity of peasant life and the flat, open landscape of eastern Europe can be seen in his unadorned yet monumental shapes. Barlach was interested in the human form and in the depiction of its interior spiritual quest.

The Transition, with its three figures enveloped in abstracted thick draperies, with minimal articulation of hands and feet is an excellent example of Barlach's style, the pose and rhythm reflecting a spiritual anguish and/or ecstasy. The delineation of the folds of the garments emphasizes the agitated bodies underneath. They symbolize the concept of a trinity; they are body, mind, and spirit. Their feet are not on the ground; they are not of this world.

The three figures form a pyramid with the apex uppermost. Thus, metaphysically from a Western Christian viewpoint, they symbolize both fire and an aspiration toward a higher unity, toward transformation (Cirlot 268). The upward movement of the three figures denotes mysticism, purification, or spiritual energy, showing us (as viewers) that at the point of transformation (a personal hardship or perhaps in the final act of death) a synthesis of self can occur allowing one to become stronger and to ascend to a new way of being.

The Transition depicts an individual's becoming, an individual's evolution through crisis and change. Importantly, it is this crisis and change that form the central core of the Grimms' tales, whether it be the sibling rivalry of *The Turnip, Aschenputtel,* and *The Queen Bee*, the dishonesty of *The Cat and Mouse in Partnership*, the curiosity of *Frau Trude,* or the inability to repent in *The Woodcutter's Child*.

Sight and Appearance

The forms of *The Transition* are abstracted; we as viewers, fill in the missing details. They are, in a sense, metaphors for characters in a European fairy tale. In the Grimms' *Aschenputtel*, the prince is young, and that is all we are told (and we assume he is handsome). Of the stepsisters we are told only that, ". . . they were beautiful and fair in appearance, but at heart were [mean] and ugly" (Junior Deluxe ed. 132). Of the hero in the Grimms' *The Queen Bee* we are told that he is called "Simpleton" (*Household Tales* 1: 269) and that his two older brothers "fell into a wild, disorderly way of living" (269). As listeners, we mentally complete these characters when we hear the story.

Barlach's *The Transition* encompasses several other European fairy-tale motifs. First of all, the figures appear to be blind and/or lost. However, perhaps it is only the outer eyes that have been blinded. The upper figure's hands are covering his eyes, implying that he may be seeing with inner eyes. The motif of blinding is common to many European fairy tales, and this blinding may be interpreted as being blind to one's nature, to one's interior reality. In the Grimms' *Aschenputtel* the two stepsisters have literally both eyes plucked out "because of their wickedness and falsehood" (Junior Deluxe ed. 142). In *Cat and Mouse in Partnership* the mouse is blind to the evil intentions of the cat. The maiden in *The Woodcutter's Child* (*Our Lady's Child*) is blind to the consequences of telling a lie. The two older brothers in *The Queen Bee* are blind to the plight of the ants, ducks, and bees. The older brother in the Grimms' *The Turnip* is so blinded with rage that "bad thoughts came to him, and he resolved to kill his brother" (*Household Tales* 2: 214). The lazy stepsister in *Mother Hulde* is blind to the consequences of her slothful and greedy ways, and the young girl in *Mother Trude* is oblivious (blind) to her parents' warning.

Religiosity, Repentance, and Rhythm

Barlach's *The Transition* exemplifies humankind's inner struggle and the search for spiritual transcendence. The profound spirituality of *The Transition* with the three figures reaching out for redemption, heads lifted upward, in an anguished prayer, resonates strongly with the Grimms' *Our Lady's* Child (in some editions translated as *The Woodcutter's Child*). Here the poor woodcutter meets a beautiful woman wearing a crown of stars. She is Mary, Queen of Heaven. She tells the woodcutter, "I am the Virgin Mary, mother of the child Jesus" (*Household Tales*1: 7). In some editions of the Grimms' tales these words are translated as, "I am the Guardian Angel of every Christian child" (Abridged ed. 70). We are in no doubt that this is a tale with an overtly Christian message. To doubly ensure that the audience clearly understands the tale's teaching, the Guardian Angel states in the last line, "Whoever will repent and confess their sins, they shall be forgiven" (73).

In *The Woodcutter's Child* the twelve mansions of Happiness (with their twelve doors) that the child may enter echo the twelve gates of the Heavenly Jerusalem, and the thirteenth mansion that the child must not enter has a similarity to the main street of the Heavenly Jerusalem which was of pure gold (Rev. 21: 15–27). When the child enters this forbidden mansion, her finger is turned to gold; it is transmuted as if by an alchemical process. Barlach's figures are flame-like; they remind us of fire, and fire has traditionally been viewed as an agent of transmutation in Western European cultures. In *The Woodcutter's Child*, the Queen is about to be burnt alive because she will not repent and admit to opening the thirteenth door (the door to the forbidden mansion, the forbidden knowledge). The fire is lit and the Queen is spiritually transformed; she gains the power to repent and confess her wrongdoing.

The mystical number three of body, mind, and spirit (Cirlot 232) is common to the European fairy tale, and we have already seen this motif as a concrete manifestation in Barlach's Expressionist sculpture *The Transition* with its three wandering souls. In *The Woodcutter's Child*, the young Queen bears three children and has three chances to recant and repent, but she refuses. Aschenputtel, who has two stepsisters, goes to the ball three nights in a row, and each night she repeats, "Little tree, little tree, shake over me, that silver and gold may come down and cover me" (Junior Deluxe ed. 137–39). Three nights in a row she also runs away from the prince. In *The Queen Bee* the youngest brother has to accomplish three tasks set down in three riddles before he can awaken the youngest princess who has two sisters. Interestingly, these three tasks correspond to the three states of matter: the ants (earth), the ducks (water), and the bees (air). Successfully completing the tasks, the youngest brother, the simpleton, marries the youngest princess, and the two older brothers marry the two older sisters.

The Quest

Emil Nolde's woodcut, *Marching Warriors* of 1917 shows two figures situated in a shallow space; they appear to be hunters or warriors. Their uncovered heads reveal their thick, vigorous hair. In a metaphysical sense, the image of the warrior symbolizes the forces that lie within the subconscious ready and waiting to come to the aid of the conscious if needed (Cirlot 364), and hair symbolizes spiritual force and growth (134–35). One figure carries a spear (a halberd), one of the three traditional weapons/attributes of the European knight (368). It is firmly and purposely clasped by the taller of the two figures, and thus may mirror an inner balance and security as outwardly the figure is firmly grounded to the earth and its energy through three points of entry: the soles of the feet and the base of the spear. These three elements form a tripod, again the mystical number three, which creates the ternary system. In the words of Lao-Tse as quoted in Cirlot, "One engenders two, two engenders three, and three engenders all things" (336).

As a Jungian archetype the spear is regarded as representative of the anima, the internal contrasexual energy of the male (368). The second figure is small, beardless, and carries no weapon. More feminine in appearance, it stands beside the tall warrior as an outward manifestation of the inner contrasexual energy. In this light, the warrior's quest can be seen as an interior spiritual journey and growth, a lifelong striving to successfully integrate and acknowledge the contrasexual energy. It is the same quest with the same dangers earlier exemplified in the Grimms' *Cat and Mouse in Partnership* and Munch's *The Kiss*. However, the reward is great, for it is the creation of the third element, the outcome or union of the masculine and feminine which resolves the conflict posed by dualism (336).

The three princes in *The Queen Bee* are on an actual quest: the older two to seek their fortunes, and the youngest to find his brothers. In the Grimms' *Frau Trude*, the little girl is on a quest to find the witch named Frau Trude. She tells her parents, "I have heard so much of Frau Trude, I will go to her some day" (*Household Tales* 1: 170). We are then told that "the maiden did not let herself be turned aside by her parent's prohibition, and still went to Frau Trude" (170). In *The Woodcutter's Child*, the quest is of a spiritual nature; the young queen's quest is to search for the means to repent.

The Great Mother Archetype

Otto Dix's lithograph, *Leonie*, of 1923 is both skeletal and ghoulish. The rouged cheeks and lipsticked mouth emphasize the figure's vanity. The large prominent teeth, red plumed hat, and red feather boa have a hint of destructive malevolence, damnation, and debased sexuality. Dix was interested in the corruptive and corrosive nature of contemporary German society. Perhaps *Leonie* is the Grimms' Frau Trude, "the witch in her proper costume" (*Household Tales* 1: 170).

Leonie's red plume sitting on top of her oversize hat, like a blazing fire, reminds us of the fire that is associated with *Frau Trude*. Interestingly, feathers are metaphysically associated with the winds and the heavens (Cirlot 102), with primal forces, and Frau Trude is the female primal force. She tells the little girl, "I have been waiting for thee, and wanting thee a long time already; thou shalt give me some light" (*Household Tales* 1: 170). Then Frau Trude changes the girl into a block of wood and throws her into the fire.

It is worth noting that the words uttered by Frau Trude perfectly illustrate Dix's concerns with the ruthlessness and violence of German society. During the First World War, Dix had been a frontline gunner in the German army and had experienced the full horror of trench warfare, including gas attacks. Thus for Dix, transcendence of reality involved transcending the base and violent aspects of humankind's struggle (Ness et al. 56–57).

So, too, Leonie's large expressive eyes looking upward toward the sky imply a hope and the possibility of salvation. They imply a possible transcendence of the defiled and decayed body. When Frau Trude changes the little girl into a block of wood and casually throws her into the fire we learn that, ". . . when it was in full blaze [the witch] sat down close to it, and warmed herself by it, and said, 'That shines bright for once in a way'" (*Household Tales* 1: 170). Literally, the little girl has transcended her body. Burned as wood she will fly up the chimney as a spark, ". . . an image of the spiritual principle which gives birth to each individual" (Cirlot 105–6), which is related to the Cabbalistic concept of souls emanating out into the world in the form of sparks (303).

Leonie also reminds us of the Grimms' *Mother Hulde*. We know that Mother Hulde has large, forebidding teeth for we are told that, "she had such great teeth that the girl was terrified and about to run away, only the old woman called her back" (Junior Deluxe ed. 145). To the good girl Mother Hulde is benevolent, showering her with gold, but to the lazy girl who pricks herself with the spindle, Mother Hulde reveals her dangerous and menacing side, the unforgiving ruthlessness of Frau Trude, for she empties a great kettle of pitch on the lazy girl. This is the lazy girl's punishment, for she has been untruthful to Mother Hulde and has tried to deceive the old woman. Thus, the lazy girl must be punished. It should be noted that throughout European history, tarring and feathering was not an uncommon form of punishment. Extremely painful it was used for public shaming and humiliation, often reserved for those who had betrayed a trust.

Leonie, *Frau Trude*, and *Mother Hulde* all reflect aspects of the "Great Mother archetype and its influence on woman's sense of identity and her awareness of the dark side of the archetype as an integral part of herself" (Lundell 75). This is the aspect of the Great Mother as Baba Yaga, Kali, and Rangda (Bly and Woodman 41). Leonie's vanity, the rouge, lipstick, and mascaraed lashes, remind us, too, of the vanity of the two stepsisters and the stepmother in the Grimms' *Aschenputtel*. They will do anything for beauty, anything to catch a man. The mother says to the one sister, "Cut the toe off [your foot] and when you are queen you will never have to go on foot" (Junior Deluxe ed. 140). To the other sister she states, "Cut a piece off your heel; when you are queen you will never have to go on foot" (141).

The Curious Girl is Kay Stone's own, modern adaptation of the Grimms' *Frau Trude* (Stone 219–37). In *The Curious Girl* the girl escapes and becomes a bird. She then travels the world collecting stories until she recognizes her own story and its importance. Thus, the feather image is common to both *Leonie* and *The Curious Girl*. By traveling on the winds of the world to collect stories for Mother Trudy the curious girl gains self-knowledge and comes to an awareness of the Great Mother archetype, in both its benevolent and malevolent aspects, as integral parts of herself.

As we have seen, there are many commonalities between the German Expressionist art pieces that were chosen for our concert at the McMaster Museum of Art, and the Grimms' tales that were told. Perhaps for us as storytellers from a Western tradition, most striking was the theme of transmutation and transformation that permeated both the works of art and the stories told and the sublimation of the exterior reality to reveal a rich and vital inner vision. Although the Grimms' tales were written a century before the German Expressionist art movement, they exhibit the same freshness and vigor, the same clarity and linearity of design, and the same concise graphic images that are reflected in the later Expressionist works. We close with a quotation from Max Luthi: "By being sublimated, all elements of the folktale [fairy tale] are so fully divested of their separate characteristics and so completely removed from the sphere in which they originated that they can come to symbolize other spheres as well" (Luthi 94).

Notes

1. The authors would like to thank the staff of the McMaster Museum of Art for encouragement and support in the preparation of this essay, and extend a special thanks to Kim G. Ness, Director and Curator, and to Gerrie Loveys, Collections and Operations Manager, for allowing the use of the reproductions of the four works cited from the McMaster Museum of Art permanent collection. We would also like to extend our thanks to today's storytellers for keeping the storytelling flame alight, and to children everywhere who have always known the value and truth of the traditional tales.
2. The opening of this story is a deathbed scene. Aschenputtel's (Cinderella's) biological mother asks her to be "good and pious." Aschenputtel mourns her mother's death by spending a great deal of time at her grave. Her father marries a woman who has two beautiful daughters who are mean and lazy. They torment Aschenputtel and insist she do all the work in the household. When her father goes away on a trip he asks his three daughters what he can bring back for them. The stepdaughters want "fine clothing" and "pearls and jewels." Aschenputtel asks her father for "the twig of the first tree that brushes your hat on your return." This is a hazel branch, which she plants on her mother's grave and waters with her tears. The tree grows and becomes home to many birds. The king of the country announces a three-day festival that all the women of the kingdom are invited to, so that the prince can pick his bride-to-be. When Aschenputtel asks to go to the festival, the stepmother gives her two seemingly impossible tasks to perform. The first one is to retrieve a bowl of lentils from the ashes in two hours. The second is to retrieve two bowls of lentils in one hour. With the help of the birds that live in the hazel tree at her mother's grave site, she is able to accomplish these tasks. Still her stepmother does not let her go to the festival. Once again the birds help to prepare Aschenputtel for each of the three days of the festival by giving her a new gown and pair of shoes to wear for each of the three days, the clothing being of progressing magnificence. The prince falls in love with Aschenputtel. Every day he tries to find out who she is, but each day she manages to escape, and although he follows her, he is not able to find out where she lives. On the final day he covers the step with pitch (or cobbler's wax) and her slipper sticks to it. Now armed with the slipper he once again tries to find Aschenputtel, his bride-to-be. Both stepsisters try to fit into the slipper by cutting off a portion of their foot; it is the birds at the mother's grave who draw the prince's attention to the fact the slipper does not fit. The prince is persistent, and he finally meets Aschenputtel; the shoe fits, and they are married. The story ends with the birds plucking out the eyes of the stepsisters because of their wickedness, and they are thus blind for the rest of their days.
3. This story is about a beautiful stepdaughter and the ugly daughter. The beautiful stepdaughter is treated poorly and is given all the chores to do. One of her duties is to spin by the well. She spins till her hands are

"bloody." As she washes the spindle in the well, she loses it. Her stepmother tells her she must recover it, and in doing so she falls into the well, finding herself in another world. In this other world, she is presented with three tasks: (one) to take some bread out of the oven that is cooked; (two) to pick apples that are ripe from a tree; (three) to keep house for Mother Hulde. She meets the challenges and shows she is both generous and kind. Mother Hulde showers her with gold when she decides to return home. The stepdaughter tells the stepmother of her experience. The stepmother wants the same wealth for her own daughter. She sends her daughter to the well, and the daughter proceeds to prick her finger with a thorn to get blood on the spindle and then drops it down the well. She then jumps down the well to retrieve the spindle. Once in the other world, the ugly daughter shows herself to be lazy and mean by refusing to perform the three tasks. Mother Hulde rewards her by covering her with pitch when she returns home.

4. *The Cat and the Mouse in Partnership* is a short story about the partnership of a cat and a mouse. The issue is the storage of their food reserve (a pot of fat). The relationship is the central focus of the story. The cat lies and pretends to protect the mouse, while the mouse trustingly takes on the role of caregiver. The story evolves with the cat visiting the church where the food is stored and gradually eating all the fat. He does not tell the mouse of his visits. When the food is needed, the mouse visits the church and discovers their supplies are gone. The mouse begins to piece together the lies and small clues the cat has left and then confronts the cat. The cat warns the mouse that if she does not let the situation be, she will be devoured. The mouse continues and accuses the cat, and the cat then eats the mouse. The last line of the story states, "And that is the way of the world."

5. *The Queen Bee* is a story of sibling rivalry. The story opens with three brothers. The two older brothers consider themselves wise and look at their younger brother as a simpleton. They are amused by the youngest brother's concern for the ants, the ducks, and the bees. The youngest brother saves all three of these creatures from the older brothers' destructive nature. His gentle and kind ways are repaid. The brothers come upon a castle where everyone is under a spell and in a deep sleep. They are given three tasks that will free the members of the court, including a beautiful princess. The older brothers both try and fail. Now the youngest brother must try not only to free all those in the castle but his brothers as well. With the help of the ants (to retrieve the princess's pearls), the ducks (to retrieve the key to the chamber that holds the princess), and the queen bee (to determine which princess has eaten honey before she has fallen asleep), the youngest brother solves the riddles and breaks the spell. He marries the princess and becomes ruler of the kingdom.

6. *The Turnip* is a story about two brothers who return from the war; one is very poor, and the other is wealthy. The poor brother takes up farming and grows an enormous turnip. This turnip is so large and so unusual that he decides to give it to the king as a gift. The king, out of sympathy and gratitude, gives the young man land and riches. The wealthier brother hears

of his brother's good fortune and decides he, too, will give the king a gift. He gives the king beautiful horses and gold in hopes of receiving even more wealth than his brother. The king rewards the second brother for his generosity by giving him the large and unusual turnip. This makes the wealthy brother very angry, and he decides to murder his poorer, simpler brother. He ambushes him, ties him up in a bag, and hangs him from the branch of a tree. The simpler brother then uses his wits to escape from the bag by exchanging places with a gullible young student.

7. A little girl, the daughter of a poor woodcutter and his wife, is taken by a beautiful woman wearing a crown to the land of happiness (heaven). Here the girl is raised in splendor but is told she cannot enter the thirteenth door in the land of happiness. She opens the door and her finger is turned to gold. She will not confess her crime to the guardian angel, so she is sent back to earth and lives for many years in a forest. A king, out hunting, discovers the maiden, falls in love with her, and marries her, making her queen. The queen bears the king three children. At the birth of each child the guardian angel appears and asks the queen if she opened the thirteenth door. Each time the queen replies that she did not, and the child is immediately taken away by the angel. The people of the kingdom believe that the queen has murdered her children, and so she is condemned to be burnt at the stake. As the fire is lit, the queen repents and confesses her sin. The children are then returned to her.

8. Kay Stone's *The Curious Girl* begins where *Mother Trude* (see note 9) ends. The young girl escapes as a spark from the fire. The witch captures her and then changes her into a bird. She allows the bird to roam the world looking for a story that has "no beginning, no end and one I [the witch] have never heard." If the girl, who is now a bird, finds a story that meets these requirements, she will be set free and return to her original form. The story ends with the curious girl in her bird form telling her own story, the story of her own life. The telling of her own story wins her freedom and restores her to human form.

9. The Grimms' *Mother Trude (Frau Trude)* is a short cautionary tale. The story begins with a curious young girl who will not listen or do as her parents ask. This girl has heard of Mother Trude and wants to visit her. Her parents forbid it, but she goes to visit the old lady anyway. Mother Trude asks the girl what she has seen. The girls answers that through the window she saw "the devil with his fiery head." Mother Trude chillingly answers, "You have seen the witch in her rightful form." She then changes the girl into a stick of wood and tosses her onto the fire.

Works Cited

Bly, Robert, and Marion Woodman. *The Maiden King: The Reunion of Masculine and Feminine.* New York: Henry Holt and Company, 1998.

Cirlot, J. E. *A Dictionary of Symbols.* 2nd ed. Jack Sage, Trans. London: Routledge & Kegan Paul, 1985.

Greenwood, Michael. "German Expressionist Prints from the Collection of McMaster University, Hamilton." *The National Gallery of Canada Journal* 8 (Oct. 1975): 1–8.

Grimm, Jakob, and Wilhelm Grimm. *Grimm's Fairy Tales.* Abridged ed. London: Dean & Son Ltd., 1948.

———. *Grimm's Fairy Tales.* Junior Deluxe ed. New York: Nelson Doubleday, Inc., 1954.

———. *Grimm's Household Tales.* 2 vols. Trans. Margaret Hunt. Detroit: Singing Tower Press, 1968.

Kane, Alice. *The Dreamer Awakes.* Peterborough: Broadview Press, 1995.

Lundell, Torborg. *Fairy Tale Mothers.* New York: Peter Lang Publishing Inc., 1990.

Luthi, Max. *The European Folktale: Form and Nature.* Bloomington: Indiana University Press, 1982.

Ness, Kim G., K. G., Watson, J. C., and N. O'Laoghaire. *The Levy Legacy.* Hamilton: McMaster Museum of Art, 1996.

Richard, Lionel. *The Concise Encyclopedia of Expressionism.* Ware: Omega Books Ltd., 1984.

Rosenberg, Jacob. "German Expressionist Printmakers." *Magazine of Art* 35 (Dec. 1945): 300–5.

Stone, Kay. *Burning Brightly: New Light on Tales Told Today.* Peterborough: Broadview Press Ltd, 1998.

Wiginton, Colin. *Geist.* Hamilton: McMaster Museum of Art, [press release], 1998.

9

Rhyme as Reason: Conjunct Verbs in Ojibwe Storytelling

Nila Friedberg

The telling of narratives is often associated with particular devices that "make the story flow." For instance, in English, Icelandic, and Russian, the verb normally follows the subject. However, in narrative contexts the verb often occurs in front of the subject instead, as shown in (1). Such a word order signals that the sentence belongs to the medium of a cohesive narrative such as a story, a novel, or a joke:

(1)
English	"I am so happy"	*said*	*she*	(Collins 31)
		Verb	Subject	

Icelandic	*Kom*	*Olafur*	seint	heim	
	came	Olaf	late	home.	
	Verb	Subject			
	"Olaf came home late"				(Sigurdsson 41)

Russian	*Prixodit Vovochka*		domoj	
	Comes Vovochka		home	
	Verb Subject			
	"Vovochka comes home"			(Babyonyshev 25)

In Ojibwe, an Algonquian language spoken in the area of the Great Lakes, North America (Kaye), storytellers create the narrative flavor by using a special verb form called the conjunct (Bloomfield 35). Researchers on Algonquian languages have long studied the fine meanings of the conjuncts in narratives (Rhodes 110–11, Dahlstrom 117–19, Starks 305,

Valentine *Amik* 400). However, what has been neglected in the literature is a possible poetic account of these forms. In this chapter,[1] I propose that the sounds at the end of conjunct verbs make them especially suited for creating memorable sound patterns. In terms of sound, the conjunct verb endings are quite restricted, whereas other verb forms in the language exhibit a greater variety of endings. Thus, conjunct verbs easily lend themselves to creating sound repetition or partial rhymes.

The suggestion that poetic devices play a role in narratives is not without precedent. Hymes (309) has argued that Native American oral performance exhibits elements of measured verse such as lines, verses, stanzas, and scenes. In view of this fact, it is not surprising that sound repetition, another poetic device, would play a role in storytelling as well.

The question as to whether conjuncts are frequent in stories because of what they mean or because of how they sound is similar to the debate about how verse is composed: "When poets write a poem, do they start with pure rhythm (i.e., form) or do they start with the actual words (i.e., meaning)?" There is no straightforward answer to this question. Sometimes, poets replace the words in a line in order to improve the rhythm, i.e., give up some aspects of meaning in favor of form, whereas at other times, the opposite situation holds. Both form and meaning considerations might govern the choice of words in a poetic composition. For this reason, the investigation of the poetic aspect of conjunct usage is as necessary as the investigation of what conjuncts mean.

The specific story analyzed in this essay is *Cahkaapehsh and the Moon*,[2] which appears in the collection of stories *Ninoontaan: I Can Hear It* written by Cecilia Sugarhead and edited by J. O'Meara. The stories in this collection are printed versions of the oral narratives the author heard while she was growing up in Landsdowne House (O'Meara 7).

Algonquian verbs can take two types of endings, which Bloomfield (35) called the independent and the conjunct. The independent ending is attached to a verb that occurs in the main clause; the conjunct ending is attached to a verb that occurs in the subordinate clause. The difference between an independent and a conjunct verb is demonstrated in (2) and (3). The verb stem *inaapi* 'look around' has the conjunct ending *-c* when it occurs in the subordinate clause in (2), but it lacks such an ending in the main clause in (3). In (2) the conjunct verb is italicized.[3]

(2) Mekwaac   tahsh   *e-inaapi-c*   o-kii-onci-waapamaan
    While   and   look-Cj   3p-past-there-see
    While he was looking around, he saw

    Wemishoohsh-an
    Wemishoohs-obv
    Wemishoohsh from up there.

(3) Ishpimink   tahsh   inaapi   kekahpii
    Into the sky   and   look-Ind   finally
    Finally she looks up into the sky   (Sugarhead 35)

Conjunct verbs are not limited to subordinate clauses and are extremely common in main clauses in narrative contexts. For example, Starks (305) reports that in Woods Cree narratives, conjuncts occur in 75 percent of main clauses, whereas in conversation, conjuncts occur only in 48 percent of main clauses.[4]

The predominance of conjuncts in narrative contexts is not surprising because main clause conjuncts indicate a close logical or temporal sequence with the preceding sentence (Rhodes 111, Valentine *Amik* 400), and sentences in a narrative are characterized by a much higher degree of cohesion than the sentences in ordinary conversation (Starks 305). Main clause conjuncts in narratives have also been reported in other Ojibwe dialects including Eastern Ojibwa (Rhodes 111), Ottawa (Rhodes 110), Pikogan Algonquin (Valentine *Amik* 400) and Golden Lake Algonquin (Aubin Three 2–3, Girls 2). The Landsdowne examples are shown in (4) and (5):

(4) Ahpan   *wententi-c*   kape-kiishik.
    Now   be away-Cj   all day
    He would be away all day long.   (Sugarhead 34)

(5) *Ci-onahtoo-waac*   aaniin   ahpii   minihkohk   ke-sookihpwahk
    fut-decide-3p.pl Cj how   when   amount   fut-snow
    They were to decide how long it would snow

    takwaaki-nk   noohpimi-nk
    be autumn-Cj   in the forest
    in the forest during the fall.   (Sugarhead 38)

The meaning and function of conjuncts in the story *Cahkaapehsh and the Moon*, written in the Landsdowne dialect of Ojibwe, are subsequently examined.

The story *Cahkaapehsh and the Moon* portrays a Cree mythical hero, Cahkaapehsh, who lived with his mother, Noohkomihs, and liked to tease people and animals. One day his mother sent him to the lake to get some water and warned him not to tease the moon. Cahkaapehsh violated the prohibition and was converted into the constellation of Aquarius.

In (6) there are some excerpts from the story:

(6a) Weshkac   miina   kihci-ihkwe   eshi-nihkaaso-kopanen
     Long ago   and   old woman   thus-name must have been
     Long ago there was an old woman whose name must have been

  Noohkomihs.
  Noohkomihs.

(b) Mii   tahsh   o-kii-ayaawa-kopan   naapenhsan
    So   and   had-Ind   boy
    She had a little boy

    eshi-nihkaasonikopanen   Cahkaapehsh.
    thus-name must have been   Cahkaapehsh
    who was called Cahkaapehsh

(c) Mii   tahsh   aha Cahkaapehsh   kii-minoki
    So   and   that-animate   past-healthy Ind
    And that Cahkaapehsh was healthy

    Kaye   kii-mashkawisii.
    And   past-strong Ind
    and strong.

(d) Mii   tahsh   miina   kaye   kii-nihtaa-papaami-ayaa
    So   and   again   also   past-travel around-Ind
    And so Cahkaapehsh would travel around a lot,

    Aha   Cahkaapehsh kaye   tahsh   kii-nihtaa-mamiihkintisi
    That   Cahkaapehsh also   and   past-like to tease-Ind
    and that Cahkaapehsh also liked to tease

awiiyan	iko	kaye	awiiyaashihshan
everybody	emph	also	animals

people and animals

kaye	piko	nipiihkaank	kaa-ayaani-c	ekwa
also	only	in the water	who-live-3p Cj	so

and anything that was in the water,

kaye anihshinaape.
And people.
and the people too.   (Sugarhead 34)

The verb phrases in sentences (6a-6d) refer to states such as "being healthy," "liking to tease animals," "having a son." They do not form a chain of successive events, as occurs in the sentence "I came, I saw, I conquered." There is neither a temporal link between these states nor is there any logical link because being healthy does not necessarily imply teasing everybody. Hence, all of the verbs in this passage are marked as independent because they are not logically or temporally linked and because they are mentioned in the story for the first time.

Conversely, consider the verbs in sentences (6e-6h), which follow sentences (6a-6d) in the original story:

(6e) | Mii | piko | kaye | kaa-ishi-wanihikaaniwatinik | *e-kii-ishaa-c* |
|---|---|---|---|---|
| And | only | also | past-thus-go to the water | past-go-3p-Cj |

And when he went down to the water, he went

e-kii-mamiihkincihtoo-c	wanihikanini	kaye	piko	nakwaakanini.
past-tease-3p.Cj	traps	and	only	snares.

and teased traps and snares.

(f) | Ahpan | *wententi-c* | kape-kiishik. |
|---|---|---|
| Now | be away-Cj | all day |

He would be away all day long.

(g) | Paanimaa | piko | e-aakwaatiipihkaanik | *e-pikiiwe-c* |
|---|---|---|---|
| Later | just | later on at night | here come-Cj |

Late in the middle of the night he would come back home.

(h) Mii   tahsh   aha   Noohkomihs   *e-kanoonaa-c* [...]
    So   and   that-anim   Noohkomihs   ask-3p-Cj
    And so Noohkomihs would ask him: (Sugarhead 34)

Sentence (6e) repeats the same verb stem as sentence (6d) *(kii-nihtaa-mamiihkintisi* 'liked to tease' versus *e-kii-mamiihkincihtoo-c* 'teased'). The repeated verb in (e) is in a conjunct form. Sentence (f) is a direct consequence of (e): Cahkaapehsh would be away because he was teasing traps and snares. The verb in (f) is marked by the conjunct as well. Sentences (f), (g), and (h) form a temporal sequence: First Cahkaapehsh would be away; then he would come home late; then Noohkomihs would ask him a question. All of the verbs are marked by the conjunct.

Thus, the type of linking found in Landsdowne Ojibwe seems quite similar to the findings of Rhodes (110–11), Valentine (*Amik* 400), and Dahlstrom (117–19); main clause conjuncts are used to signal a temporal or logical link to the previous sentence. The linking function of conjuncts seems entirely consistent with their distribution in the language. Speakers use conjuncts in stories because conjuncts are associated with subordinate clauses. That is to say, in the same way as a subordinate clause has a tight connection to the main clause, the main clause employing a conjunct has a tight connection to the preceding narrative.

Note, however, that the use of main clause conjuncts is not the only way to indicate the connection between sentences in the narrative. One can achieve the same linking effect by using various discourse particles such as *mii tahsh* 'and so' (which can precede either an independent or a conjunct verb in Landsdowne), *ahpan* 'now' and so on. One can also signal linking by omitting overt noun phrases, as in (6e-6g).

Whereas main clause conjuncts express the connection between sentences, one still has to explain why this particular method of linking is chosen by the author so frequently.

One possibility is that conjuncts serve a special poetic function. Conjuncts create sound repetition (or consonance or partial rhymes) more easily than independent verbs. Most of the conjuncts in the Landsdowne text end in the same sound c (as in "*ch*air"); in contrast, independent verbs exhibit a greater variety of endings:[5]

(7) *Conjunct verbs in the story (2 types of final sounds, -c and -k)*
    e-kii-ishaa-**c**   e-kii-mamiihkincihtoo-**c**   wententi-**c**
    went   teased   is away

    e-pi-kiiwe-**c**   e-kanoonaa-**c** e-kwiinawi-piihaa-**c**
    comes back   asks   is tired of waiting

    ehkito**c**   e-noohsahanaa-**c**   eshi-kiishkihkawe-**c**
    says   tracks down   leave one's tracks cut off

    e-ayinaapi-**c**   e-ahteni-**k**
    looks around   be there

(8) *Independent verbs in the story (5 types of final sounds)*
    kii-minok-**i**   kii-mashkawis-**ii**   kii-nihtaa-papaami-ay-**aa**
    past-healthy Ind   past-strong Ind   past-skill- around-have Ind

    kii-nihtaa-mamiihkintis-**i**   inaap-**i**   o-kii-waapa-m-aa-**n**
    past-skill-tease   looks-Ind   3p-past-see-anim-him Ind

    kii-macenta-**m**
    past-sad-Ind

To make the claim more explicit, the conjunct is especially suited for creating sound repetition for two reasons. First, the third person singular and plural forms of the independent verbs in (9) end with two different sounds (-*o* versus -*k*), whereas the conjunct verbs in (10) end with the same sound:[6]

(9) *Independent*
    he says   ihkit-**o**
    they say   ihkitowa-**k**

(10) *Conjunct*
    that he says   ihkito-**c**
    that they say   ihkitowaa-**c**

Second, the distinction between final sounds that exists in the independent verbs is often neutralized in the conjunct:

Table 1. Independent Verbs

ihkit*o*	pimohs*e*	ayaawaa*n*	maw*i*
he says	he walks by	he has	he cries

Table 2. Conjunct Verbs

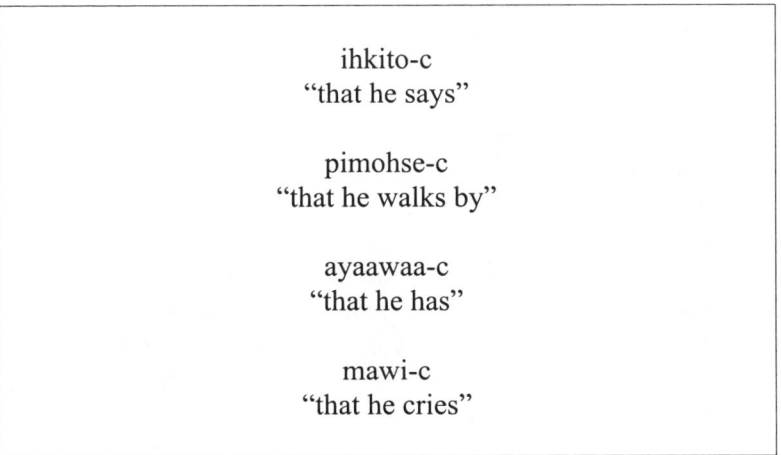

One might claim that the repetition of the ending -*c* in the story is not a matter of the narrator's choice because this is the only way conjuncts can be expressed in the third person. However, the author is free to choose between an independent and a conjunct verb. Thus, choosing the conjunct implies the option of repeating the same sound.

What effect does the repetition of -*c* create? This repetition is best explained by the fact that Ojibwe stories are intended to be performed. By using the forms exhibiting partial rhymes, the storyteller directs the attention of the audience toward the verbs. The identical endings of these verbs create the same effect as identical clothes on two siblings: they capture our attention and emphasize the fact that the siblings are related. The reason the storyteller might want to draw the attention of the audience toward verbs is obvious: It is verbs that constitute the core of the plot because stories typically depict a limited number of heroes performing numerous actions.

Various researchers (Hymes 309, Valentine *Amik* 387) have suggested that Native American narratives exhibit elements of measured verse, such as lines, verses, stanzas, and scenes. The division into these elements is based on the repeated use of discourse particles (such as *mii* 'so' in Ojibwe), syntactic parallelism, and many other rhetorical devices (Valentine *Amik* 387–427). I have shown an additional reason for considering Native American storytelling, or at least Ojibwe storytelling, as a form of poetry: Apart from the repetition of discourse particles, narratives also exhibit the repetition of sound.

Sound repetition performs a poetic function in Ojibwe, and hence one may wonder why readers of English prose do not notice the repetition of the present tense ending -*s*, even though it occurs extremely often. The reason is that in Ojibwe the same verb can be expressed in two competing ways: The conjunct and the independent. In English, there are no other options besides "walks"; -*s* is the only way in which the present tense can be expressed for the third person singular. In other words, sound repetition only plays a role in those languages where there is a distinct possibility of not using it.

The suggested account of the conjunct usage sheds light on the function of narrative constructions in English and other Indo-European languages. Similar to Ojibwe, the repetition of "said she" and "said he" in English narratives creates rhymes,[7] and may be frequent in novels for poetic reasons. Moreover, the use of the special verb-subject word order in the English, Russian, and Icelandic narratives may serve a poetic function as well, because such a word order creates syntactic parallelism.

Therefore, across languages, the choice of narrative constructions may be governed by poetic considerations. Such constructions are likely to contribute to the repetition of structure (syntactic parallelism) or the repetition of sound (rhyming). The validity of this hypothesis is a subject for future research.

Notes

1. This research was supported by the Graduate Research Grant from the Department of Linguistics at the University of Toronto. I am grateful to my teacher, Theresa Morin, who introduced me to the Algonquin language and inspired me to pursue the study of Algonquian linguistics. Special thanks to Alana Johns as well as to David Beck, Elan Dresher, Nigel Fabb, Deborah James, Daniel Hall, Kristin Hanson, Paul Kiparsky, John O'Meara, John Nichols, Richard Rhodes, Milan Rezac, Keren Rice, Benjamin Shaer, and Randolph Valentine.
2. I adopt the transcription system used in Sugarhead (14). In this system, "*c*" represents the sound as in "*chair*," "*sh*" represents the sound as in "*shoe*," "*y*" represents the sound as in "*yes*." Vowel length is indicated by double vowels (e.g., "*ii*").
3. My gloss is based on O'Meara's dictionary at the end of the Sugarhead collection. The following abbreviations are used: Cj — conjunct, Ind — independent; p — person, pl — plural; fut — future. Some grammatical information irrelevant to this chapter has been omitted.
4. Cree is a language that is related to Ojibwe.
5. The sound repetition discussed in this essay is quite different from the sound patterns typically found in European verse. As Hanson and Kiparsky state, "for rhyme or alliteration to become a principle of verse structure, the interval of recurrence must be measured by some other linguistic element ... defining where the alliterating or rhyming equivalences must be found" (33). The repeated instances of the sound -*c* in Ojibwe are not separated from each other by an equal number of syllables, stresses, or words.
6. I focus on the third person here because it is the most frequently used form in narratives. The same generalization holds true of other persons.
7. Thanks to Milan Rezac for bringing this point to my attention.

Works Cited

Aubin, George. "Three Texts in Golden Lake Algonquin." *Papers of the Eighteenth Algonquian Conference.* Ed. W. Cowan. Ottawa: Carleton University Press, 1987. 1–6.

———. "Girls Hunting Groundhogs:" A Text in Golden Lake Algonquin." *Papers of the Nineteenth Algonquian Conference.* Ed. W. Cowan. Ottawa: Carleton University Press, 1988. 1–5.

Babyonyshev, Maria. "Structural Connections in Syntax and Processing: Studies in Russian and Japanese." Ph.D. Diss. MIT, 1996.

Bloomfield, Leonard. *Eastern Ojibwe: Grammatical Sketch, Texts and Word List.* 1956. Toronto: University of Toronto Press, 1997.

Collins, Chris. *Local Economy.* Cambridge: MIT Press, 1997.

Dahlstrom, Amy. "Narrative Structure of a Fox Text." Eds. John D. Nichols and Arden C. Ogg. *Nikotwâsik iskwâhtêm, pâskihtêpayih! Studies in Honour of C.H. Wolfart.* Winnipeg: Algonquian and Iroquoian Linguistics, 1996. 115–32.

Hanson, Kristen, and Paul Kiparsky. "The Nature of Verse and Its Consequences for the Mixed Form." Ph.D. Diss. Stanford University and UC Berkeley, 1999.

Hymes, Dell. "Discovering Oral Perfomance and Measured Verse in American Indian Narrative." *In Vain I Tried to Tell You: Essays in Native American Ethnopoetics.* Philadelphia: University of Pennsylvania Press, 1981. 308–41.

James, Deborah. "Foreground and Background in Moose Cree Narratives." *Proceedings of the Seventeenth Algonquian Conference.* Ed. W. Cowan. Ottawa: Carleton University Press, 1986. 155–71.

Kaye, Jonathan. "The Algonquian Languages of Canada." *The Languages of Canada.* Ed. Jack Chambers. Montreal: Didier, 1979. 20–53.

Maling, Joan, and Annie Zaenen. *Syntax and Semantics: Modern Icelandic Syntax.* San Diego: Academic Press, 1990.

Nichols, John D., and Arden C. Ogg. *Nikotwâsik iskwâhtêm, pâskihtêpayih! Studies in Honour of C. H. Wolfart.* Winnipeg: Algonquian and Iroquoian Linguistics, 1996.

O'Meara, John, ed. Introduction. *Ninoontaan: I Can Hear It.* C. Sugarhead. Winnipeg: Algonquian and Iroquoian Linguistics, 1996.

Rhodes, Richard. "Some Aspects of Ojibwe Discourse." *Proceedings of the Tenth Algonquian Conference.* Ed. W. Cowan. Ottawa: Carleton University Press, 1979.

Sigurdsson, Halldor A. "V1 Declaratives and Verb Raising in Icelandic." *Syntax and Semantics: Modern Icelandic Syntax.* Eds. J. Maling and A. Zaenen. San Diego: Academic Press, 1990. 41–70.

Starks, Donna. "Planned vs. Unplanned Discourse: Oral Narrative vs. Conversation in Woods Cree." *Canadian Journal of Linguistics* 39.4 (1994): 297–320.

Sugarhead, Cecilia. *Ninoontaan: I Can Hear It*. Ed. J. O'Meara. Winnipeg: Algonquian and Iroquoian Linguistics, 1996.

Valentine, Randolph J. "Amik Anicinaabewigoban: Rhethorical Structures in Albert Mowatt's Telling of an Algonquin Tale." Eds. J. D. Nichols and A. C. Ogg. *Nikotwâsik iskwâhtêm, pâskihtêpayih! Studies in honour of C. H. Wolfart*. Winnipeg: Algonquian and Iroquoian Linguistics, 1996. 387–427.

———. "Berens River Ojibwe Rhetorical Structure." Ph.D. Diss. University of Texas at Austin, 1986.

10

Voices, Morals, and Identity in the Conversational Narratives of Ten-to-Twelve-Year-Olds

Janet Maybin

Narrative provides an enormously important resource for children who are trying to understand and explain the events they observe and take part in. Like adults, they use conversational stories to relate their experiences to others, exchange ideas, explain events, argue, or simply entertain one another and pass the time. Labov (366) shows that these narratives have both a referential function in recounting the past and also an evaluative function in that any account is also aimed at depicting what happened from a particular point of view. Often stories convey explicit or implicit moral judgments about the actions of individuals and the unfolding of events. Telling stories about these events and their own role in them, or giving their view of what happened, enables children to try out different versions of experience and of themselves. This exploration and experimentation is an important part of children's conceptual and social development. For instance, studies of young children have demonstrated that listening to and telling narratives of personal experience play an important part in children's emotional development and that they often present personal characteristics, like bravery, through comparing their own actions or reactions with those of another child in the story. In addition to the story content, the reaction of the child's audience will influence their sense of their own selfhood and of their power to affect others. The comments of listeners, the way they later weave elements of the story into their own talk, and their willingness to give conversational space and attention to particular kinds of accounts will all affect the storyteller's feelings about what they have told and the way they tell stories in the future. Finally, if we see language as mediating between the individual and their cultural environment, children learn and try out cultural values through telling and listening to stories, and the way they learn to relate events, account for experience, and represent others and themselves will all be colored and shaped by their particular cultural environment.

In this chapter I will focus on four stories told by ten-to-twelve-year-olds, two boys and two girls, who are at the transition point of moving from childhood into adolescence. These stories are part of a corpus of recorded data from an ethnographic study of children's informal language and literacy practices in two British Middle Schools in nearby working-class housing estates about fifty miles from London (Maybin, "Children's" 280–82; Maybin, "Framing" 459). The stories reflect their narrators' experiences within school, families, and peer group activities in this particular cultural environment, but they also provide an opportunity for the children to question those experiences, to problematize the way they observe people behaving, and to reflect, albeit briefly and fleetingly, on what kind of person they want to be. I shall look in particular at a feature of the stories which I would argue is central to their evaluative function, that is, the children's taking on of other people's voices. Almost all the stories in my data involved reported dialogue, and it is through taking on and reproducing the voices of others, as well as representing their own voice in particular ways, that the children are able not just to recount their experience but also to explore the issues it raises for them and to try out their own moral judgments. The children's management of these voices is quite complex. It is not just how children represent and reproduce individual voices in the stories that is significant but also the ways in which, whether consciously or unconsciously, they manipulate the relationships between voices within the stories, and the relationships between voices in the stories and previous or subsequent voices in the surrounding conversation. In order to understand the meaning of what is happening in the story and the overall meaning of the story within its conversational context, we need to look at the dialogic relationships between these different voices (Bakhtin *Speech* 92).

The Children's Stories

The stories that follow come from my interviews with the children in friendship pairs. Children frequently used narratives to explain to me about their homes, families, and out-of-school activities. The kinds of dialogue and reported speech represented in these particular stories are also found across the data.

Terri's Baby

First and most straightforwardly, children use reproduced voices to move the action forward, to give a sense of immediacy and grab the audience's attention, drawing them into the story. In the first extract below, Nicole is eleven and Karlie is twelve years old. Nicole has just told me that her sixteen-year-old sister recently had a baby, and Karlie uses an evaluative comment, "She did the best thing about it," to invite Nicole to tell me the story, which Karlie already knows well:

1	Karlie	She did the best thing about it, though, didn't she, Nicole?
2	Nicole	She didn't tell a soul, no one, that she was pregnant
3	Karlie	Until she was due, when she got into hospital, then she told them
4	Nicole	On Saturday night she had pains in her stomach, and, come the
5		following Sunday, my mum was at work and my sister come to the pub
6		and my Aunt Ella was in it and my sister went in there and said "I've got
7		pains in my stomach!" so my Aunt Ella went and got my mum, and took
8		her to the hospital, and my mum asked her if she was due on and she
9		said "No, I've just come off," and when they got her to hospital they
10		said "Take her to Maternity!" My mum was crying.
11	Janet	Your mum didn't realize she was pregnant?
12	Nicole	No, and my mum slept with her when she was ill!
13	Karlie	My dad said she did, Terri did the best thing about it. Her sister's Terri.
14	Nicole	Or if she did tell, as she's so young, she weren't allowed to have him.

The three pieces of reported speech in Nicole's story each play a vital role in unfolding the plot. "I've got pains in my stomach!" (lines 6–7) articulates the problem and sets off the train of events; "No, I've just come off" (line 9) (i.e., just finished menstruating) adds to the deepening mystery and suspense, and "Take her to Maternity!" (line 10) reveals the dramatic outcome. The urgency of the voices draws the listener in, heightening the suspense and confronting her with the contradiction between Terri's apparent lack of pregnancy symptoms, ("I've just come off") and the verdict of the hospital ("Take her to Maternity!"). It is this dynamic between Terri's voice and the voice of the hospital staff which is central to the point of the story and creates the impact of a dramatic event which is unusual and "tellable." However, the relationship between these two voices within the story is also framed by the overall evaluative slant given by Karlie's comment (appropriated from her father) that Terri "did the best thing about it" (lines 1 and 13). From this point of view, Terri's response "I've just come off" could be interpreted as part of the concealment of her pregnancy, which the girls see as sensible and admirable because otherwise "as she's so young, she weren't allowed to have him" (line 14). While the relationship between the reproduced voices within the story provides the dynamic that drives it forward, the additional relationship between these voices and comments by Karlie and Nicole in the conversation around the story are central to the evaluative point the girls are making about the wisdom of Terri's concealment.

The Bird's Nest and the Stray Cat

A similar interplay between voices within and around stories occurs in the next example, my interview with Lee (eleven years old) and Geoffrey (ten years old). Lee and Geoffrey were intensely interested in animals and birds, but they were also aware of the contrast between their own rather gentle and caring approach and the attitude of some other children.

1	Lee	Yesterday I was on, I was walking with my mum, we walked past this
2		bush, and there was this nest and it was fallen down on the floor, and I
3		goes "Mum look, there's a nest on the floor," and I goes "Mum can I go
4		and have a look at it?" and I went over there and there was four baby chicks
5		in it, little chicks, I think they were willow warbler and my mum said

6		"Climb up and put them back in the tree," so and I had some bread, eaten
7		some bread, so I fed it bits of bread, cause she had to go to the phone, and
8		em she waited and I put it back up in the tree and its mum's with it now.
9		Yea, cause someone, someone had pulled the nest down, out of the tree
10	Geoff	I know this kid called Richie Binns who knocked a nest down on purpose
11	Lee	They'd probably be dead by now
12	Geoff	three little birds in there, one of them got thrown in my court and got
13		squashed, one of them got dumped in a bush and that got squashed, and
14		one got run over.
15	Jan	Aah, that's a shame
16	Geoff	And I spent all that time putting worms and that in the nest, put it up in the
17		tree, Richie Binns knocked it back down again. That's, then, that's when
18		they got squashed.
19	Lee	The ones I found yesterday are probably dead by now cause this girl I
20		know called Ellie goes to (name of school) she'll probably nick them,
21		cause she loves birds.

22		I know someone called Alan Horton, whenever he sees a bird's nest he
23		climbs up the tree and goes "There's eggs in it" and takes the whole bird's
24	Geoff	nest into his shed, gets the eggs and smashes them with a hammer

Within Lee's initial story, he creates a polite, caring voice for himself (lines 3–4), and a kind, helpful response from his mother (line 6). The whole tenor of the story is calm and gentle, as Lee and his mother weave their activities amicably together, and the nest of chicks is safely returned to the mother bird. In the ensuing conversation, however, Lee's solicitous behavior is contrasted with that of Richie Binns, who knocks nests out of trees on purpose (line 10), Ellie, who kills with kindness (line 19–21), and the vicious hammer-wielding Alan Horton (line 22–24). Lee's voice in the story contrasts sharply with Alan Horton's reported gruff "There's eggs in it" (line 23) before he smashes them up. Children often gain a sense of their own identities through differentiating themselves from others, and while Geoffrey's animation of Alan Horton enables him to briefly explore this different, more violent version of masculinity, Geoffrey is clearly positioning himself as different from Alan and similar to Lee. Through the repeated contrasts, Lee and Geoffrey seem almost overanxious to reassure themselves that their own response is the morally correct one. While nurturing behavior like Lee's was usually accepted and applauded in talk among the girls, it was less common in conversations between boys, and it may be that Lee and Geoffrey are talking about aspects of themselves which do not fit easily into the powerful cultural conceptions of masculinity (Connell 76–81). They, therefore, have to define themselves *against* the images of Richie Binns and Alan Horton and to distinguish their own knowledgeable kindness clearly from Ellie's implied fond incompetence.

In this case, the dialogic relationship between Lee's gentle, caring voice within the story and Alan Horton's voice reproduced by Geoffrey shortly afterward is central to the evaluative point of the story, concerning the appropriate way of treating helpless creatures (and perhaps how boys should express gentleness). There is also a further dialogic relationship that underpins the evaluation in Lee's story. This is the relationship between the story about the bird's nest and a story told by Geoffrey twelve minutes earlier in the interview. Geoffrey's earlier story, reproduced below, provided a similar account of help given to a lost animal, and presented a similarly warm, supportive relationship between mother and son:

Geoff   There was this black stray cat who started coming into our garden for two nights

Lee   Is it really scruffy?

Geoff   Yea, and it didn't have no collar. It had no collar, and it had white bits at the paws, right on the paws and it had little white under there, and every night when it came into our garden we thought "Oh, we got no food for it, all we got is dog food," cause we've only got a dog, and I said to my mum "Mum, do you want me to go to the shops or will it be closed?" and she said "I think it'll be closed, it's nine o'clock!" (*laughter*)

Janet   So what did you do?

Geoff   I thought "Em, do cats like bread?" cause I had a few sandwiches, and my mum said "That one might, you never know," so I gave it a bit of bread and it eat a bit, it eat a bit, only a little bit

The similarity between the two stories is not just in the content matter but also in the way they are structured. In both cases, the complicating action starts with a problem described in dialogue, followed by a polite request to Mum. Mum then offers helpful advice, and Geoffrey or Lee give the cat or bird some bread. Both stories end with a rhythmic three-part list: "it eat a bit, it eat a bit, only a little bit" and "I had some bread, eaten some bread, so I fed it bits of bread." Lee's moral alignment with his friend is thus expressed through the theme and structure of his story, including the almost poetic echo at the end. The striking similarities between the two stories are shown in the following table:

Table 1. Comparison of *The Stray Cat* and *The Bird's Nest*

The Stray Cat	The Bird's Nest	
we thought "Oh, we got no food for it, all we got is dog food,"	I goes "Mum look, there's a nest on the floor,"	*problem*
"Mum, do you want me to go to the shops or will it be closed?"	"Mum can I go and have a look at it?"	*request*
I thought "Em, do cats like bread?" cause I had a few sandwiches, and my mum said "That one might, you never know,"	my mum said "Climb up and put them back in the tree,"	*advice*
so I gave it a bit of bread and it eat a bit, it eat a bit, only a little bit	and I had some bread, eaten some bread, so I fed it bits of bread,	*giving bread*

Lee's whole story is an echo of Geoffrey's earlier one, expressing approval of Geoffrey's actions and presenting a positive evaluation of their relationship. Bakhtin (*Speech* 92) argues that everything we say or write is some kind of response and is also shaped in anticipation of its own possible responses. An utterance or text always, therefore, always faces two ways: backward toward previous utterances and forward toward its own audience. Thus, Lee's story faces back toward Geoffrey's and forward toward how he anticipates that Geoffrey and I may respond. Both I and Geoffrey heard and evaluated Lee's story about the bird's nest in the light of having heard Geoffrey's story about the stray cat only twelve minutes before. This mirroring of themes and structures in conversational stories is important in the development and consolidation of women's friendships (Coates 83–9). Not surprisingly, there is a similar process going on in Lee and Geoffrey's conversation, which confirms their shared moral position and their relationship.

Michelle's Dad

In the children's talk there were often linked chains of stories, as one child would respond to a friend's narrative by recounting their own, or a narrator would relate a number of stories around a central theme. My final example focuses on a child's attempt to understand family conflict expressed through the relationship among the voices of her mother, her father, and herself, over a series of linked stories. In my interview with Michelle and Kim (both eleven years old), they told a number of stories about whether people were treated justly and fairly in various incidents in school and at home. These included accounts by Michelle about her father, who had moved out when Michelle was five but who kept coming back and abusing her mother. In the first extract below, Michelle recounts one incident where her father's violence and power are portrayed through the voice she creates for him, with her mother's and her own voice also playing a central role in the representation and interpretation of events.

1	Michelle	He's jealous, you know you can get men jealous but they're allowed
2		to go with someone else but if they find out their wife's got someone
3		else and they've left . . . Cause my mum, she, she had some
4		boyfriends and he, he caught her out once and he done her really
5		badly, smashed all the pipes in her stomach
6	Janet	What, what, your dad?
7	Michelle	Cause he can be nasty when he wants to . . . We've got a massive telly
8		in our front room and all furniture we've got new and it, my mum
9		run out once cause he whacked the phone right round her face, she
10		just run out the back, so did I cause I'm more, I love my dad, I love

Voices, Morals, and Identity

11		them both but I'm close to my dad, but, if he lays a hand on her I'm
12		on my mum's side, do you know what I mean? So I run out with
13		her, and em, we sat down outside the front with Ann and all that
14		this man thought he was well hard, the other boys called him out the
15		house, he sat out there, and when my dad come out and he (dad)
16		goes "You try to stick up for my wife, I'll have you all on," you
17		know, beat 'em all up and all the men walked in their house and shut
18		the door. So my dad goes to my mum "Right, see you later, I'm
19		going to smash your telly" and he pretended to smash that he goes
20		"I'll see you later I'm going to smash your furniture in half." And
21		my mum was kind of going "If you don't get in here I will do it" and
22		all that. I said "Mum, just go in there and I'll stay with ya" so I
23		walked in there with them and he didn't touch her at all
24	Kim	He won't touch her with, if Michelle's there because

25	Michelle	Yes cause I'm his favorite . . . I'm closest to my dad, like all girls
26		mostly are, cause my mum's closer to her dad

In this extract, the danger and violence of the situation are given impact and immediacy through the voices of Michelle's parents. Her father's three utterances; "You try to stick up for my wife, I'll have you all on" (line 16–17), "Right, see you later, I'm going to smash your telly" (line 19) and "I'll see you later I'm going to smash your furniture in half" (lines 20–21) build up the tension and suspense of the situation, and Michelle's mother echoes his anger and violence in her "If you don't get in here I will do it" (21–22). The relationship between these voices conveys the tenor of the parents' relationship, and the representation of this heated exchange provides a dramatic contrast with the practical, authoritative tone of Michelle's own statement "Mum, just go in there and I'll stay with ya," and presents her successful intervention as all the more remarkable.

As in the previous examples, the evaluative force of the story is shaped by earlier comments in the conversation. In this case, the story about Michelle's father's threats to her mother is heard in the light of Michelle's comments about her father's violence, jealousy, and "nastiness." Michelle's own evaluative position, however, is not straightforward. Her alignment as narrator seems to be with her mother, and perhaps with women more generally, in her framing comments "He's jealous you know you can get men jealous but they're allowed to go with someone else" (line 1) and "he can be nasty when he wants to" (line 7). However, she also states twice that she is close, or closer, to her Dad (lines 11 and 25). Further, her description of how all the neighborhood men are frightened of him suggests a certain pride. Again, though, she justifies her closeness with her father partly by comparing it with her mother's relationship with Michelle's grandfather: "I'm closest to my dad, like all girls mostly are, cause my mum's closer to her dad" (lines 25–26). The alignment as narrator with her mother is produced even more clearly in the next extract when Michelle explains her mother's response to the doctor's suggestion that she should take her husband to court:

1	Michelle	But my dad can get nicked cause the doctor see all the bruises over her
2		and he says "Who's done this?" and he found out and it's on his
3		records, you know they keep records, so he retyped it out again, she
4		goes to the doctor's about crying all day with the bruises. He said that
5		we'll go and get him done and she said "Don't, don't" cause when he
6		comes out here she doesn't want to do him any more cause she's
7		really scared of him . . . but he said from now on he won't lay a hand on
8		her, but that's a lie my mum said.

In line 5, Michelle moves from direct reporting of her mother's speech, "Don't don't," into a short stretch of discourse, which belongs grammatically to her own voice as narrator but is strongly colored emotionally by her mother's voice: "cause when he comes out here she doesn't want to do him any more cause she's really scared of him" (lines 5–7). The empathy is even clearer in the oral recording, where Michelle's voice tone echoes her mother's fear, and we can hear both Michelle's voice and her mother's, simultaneously. This kind of double-voicing (Bakhtin *Problems* 189) has also been termed "free indirect discourse" (Toolan 122–25) where, although the third person is used, the story time is foregrounded, and the character's emotional state is dominant. Thus Michelle refers to her mother as "she," but "here" means her mother's home, and "she doesn't want" and "she's really scared" directly reflect her mother's state of mind. This, double-voicing can be used by narrators to express a temporary alignment, in words, value, and perspective, of the narrator with a character, thus conveying the character's internal feelings and temporally merging their voice and evaluative perspective with the narrator's.

The contradiction between Michelle's statements about her closeness to her father and her contrasting evaluative alignment with her mother reflects the dilemma of loving both of two warring parents, whose relationship colors Michelle's negotiation of her own gendered identity as she moves from childhood into adolescence. It is the conflict between her parents' voices that carries the evaluative function of the narratives and enables Michelle to momentarily try on her father's strength and violence as well as her mother's anger and fear. She positions herself in relation to her parents' perspectives both through explicit statements and through focalization. While aligning herself in terms of gender with her mother ("you can get men jealous"), she appears to portray herself as more powerful than her mother and manages to express attachment to her father without condoning his behavior.

Reproduced voices in the children's stories drive the action and fuel the moral dilemmas they are exploring, whether it is the wisdom of concealing a pregnancy, the choice to nurture or destroy baby birds, or how to understand a father's violence. The animation of voices within the stories enables children to try out different perspectives. For example, Geoffrey represents his own voice as caring but briefly takes on the violence of Alan Horton, whereas Michelle tries out both her mother's and her father's anger. More significantly, I have suggested that children's manipulation of the relationship between voices provides them with the opportunity to explore and question issues raised by their experience. The contradiction between Terri's voice and what "they" said at the hospital provides Karlie and Nicole with the space to evaluate Terri's actions. Geoffrey and Lee's echoing of each other's voices and the contrast they draw with Alan Horton's helps them to consolidate their own moral assessment of how small, helpless animals should be treated. For Michelle, the irreconcilable conflict between her parents echoes through the account to her reporting of their conflicting voices right at the end: "But he said from now on he won't lay a hand on her, but that's a lie my mum said." The relationship between her parents' voices, her own voice inside the account, and the relationship of these voices with her narrator's voice enable Michelle to express and briefly explore the conflict between her personal attachment to her father and her moral alignment with her mother.

I have shown how stories are also responses to previous stories and other conversations. Lee's story echoes Geoffrey's, and Karlie uses her father's response to hearing the story of Terri's pregnancy on a previous occasion to frame and evaluate its new telling in the interview with myself. The two extracts from Michelle, together with the other accounts she told during the interview, built up a cumulative picture of her parents' behavior which was also framed by the stories about justice and fairness told by Michelle and Kim earlier in the interview. Thus, a network of intertextual links between stories told within a conversation or on different occasions is developed so that the meaning of an utterance by any particular voice in a story, and the meaning and evaluative function of the story as a whole, resonate with the connotations of dialogic relations with other stories and conversations.

The narratives analyzed here raise themes that occur across the talk I recorded, concerning issues of care and cruelty, children's changing relationships with parents and other authority figures, and how to take on the gendered identities and relationships of men and women. Individual stories can be seen as one turn in what might be called "long conversations" between children, about the business of moving from childhood into adolescence in a particular cultural setting and about their own emerging identities and agency. These "long conversations" are carried on in different contexts across days and weeks as children return again and again to the themes that are important to them, revisiting and exploring the issues in different stories and exchanges and from different perspectives, through the animation and dialogic work of reported voices.

Works Cited

Bakhtin, Michael. *Problems of Dostoevsky's Poetics.* Trans. and ed. C. Emerson. Minneapolis: University of Minnesota Press, 1984.
———. *Speech Genres and Other Late Essays.* Ed. Caryl Emerson and Michael Holquist. Austin: University of Texas Press, 1986.
Coates, Jennifer. *Women Talk: Conversation Between Women Friends.* Oxford: Blackwell, 1996.
Connell, Robert. *Masculinity.* London: Polity, 1995.
Labov, William. *Language in the Inner City.* Philadelphia: University of Philadelphia Press, 1972.
Maybin, Janet. "Children's Voices: Talk, Knowledge and Identity." *The Sociolinguistics Reader, Vol. 2: Gender and Discourse.* Eds. J. Cheshire and P. Trudgill. London: Edward Arnold, 1998. 278–94.
———. "Framing and Evaluation in 10–12 Year Old School Children's Use of Appropriated Speech, in Relation to Their Induction into Educational Procedures and Practices." *TEXT* 19.4 (1999): 459–84.
Toolan, Michael. *Narrative: A Critical Linguistic Introduction.* London: Routledge, 1988.

11

A Man Amongst Men: The Intersection of Verbal, Visual, and Vocal Elements in an Oral Narrative

Joan Swann

In this essay I present an analysis of an oral narrative told by a professional storyteller, Jan Blake.[1] The story is one of four recorded in front of a live audience in the southeast of England. Jan Blake was born in Manchester but now lives in London. Her parents came to England from Jamaica. Many of the stories she tells are from the Caribbean or from Africa, but there is no tradition of storytelling in her family. Jan built up her repertoire of stories from contacts with other storytellers and from reading and research.

The story I want to focus on is believed to have come from Nigeria. It is entitled *A Man Amongst Men*. Like others in Jan's repertoire, the story forms part of an oral tradition, but it has also been included in a written collection of African folktales (Abrahams 86–89). The stories in Abrahams' collection have different sources—some come from the records of nineteenth-century missionaries and others from more recent recordings by anthropologists and folklorists. Abrahams does not give a specific source for his version of *A Man Amongst Men*. More importantly, it was originally oral but was transcribed and later rewritten for popular audiences. Abrahams comments that he has made the stories in his collection more "appropriate" for this context. For instance, he has cut out repetitions and hesitations that would be more fitting in an oral performance as well as corrected the overliterary style of some nineteenth-century written versions.

Abrahams, like many folklorists, emphasizes the original context for his stories, the fact that they have been told at the fireside or in the family compound, known by people in the community, often alluding to some of those present (e.g., praising a chief or taunting someone judged to have done wrong): ". . . they embody the inherited wisdom—social, personal, and moral—of the people whose world we see through the filter of folklore" (xvi). Whereas Jan recreates an oral version of one of these stories, this is clearly also subject to considerable recontextualization—as a performance by a professional British storyteller whose audience does not know her and is unfamiliar both with the story itself and the traditions it represents.[2]

The story concerns a powerful hunter, termed a "man amongst men" because of the respect he receives. One day, the hunter's wife goes to the well but finds she can't draw up the calabash at the bottom of the well. Another woman arrives and asks her baby to draw up the calabash. The baby is tremendously strong and fills calabashes both for his mother and the hunter's wife. The hunter's wife learns that this is the son of another "man amongst men." That night she tells her husband, who becomes very worried about the existence of another man amongst men. The next morning the hunter goes with his wife to the well but finds he is unable to draw up the calabash. Once again, the other woman arrives with her baby, who fills both calabashes. The hunter does not heed warnings from this woman and insists on accompanying her home to meet her husband. Once there, he realizes that the husband is a giant, much larger and more powerful than he is. The hunter hides when the giant comes home to eat and tries to escape while the giant is sleeping. The giant wakes, however, and chases the hunter. During the chase, the hunter passes a group of villagers hoeing land and later a group of men building a house. Both groups offer to help him, but they flee on seeing the giant approach. Eventually, the hunter encounters another, equally powerful giant. The two giants fight, and, because they are equally matched, they eventually hammer one another into the ground. The hunter escapes, vowing never again to say he is a "man amongst men." They say that, whenever there's an earthquake, this is because of the two giants fighting under the ground to decide who is the man amongst men.

At an impressionistic level, *A Man Amongst Men* comes across, like Jan's other stories, as being highly action-packed. The story is about a sequence of events that follow on rapidly from one another. It does not contain long descriptive passages, and while we do learn something of the characters' personalities and emotional states, this is not complex. The hunter and the two giants are vain and boastful and not terribly bright. In one way or another, they all get their comeuppance. The hunter's wife and the first giant's wife are long-suffering but smarter than their husbands in that they successfully foretell their respective husband's downfall. The characters can almost be regarded as stock characters, with character development limited to the hunter "learning his lesson."

My interest in the story, and in Jan's storytelling in general, however, lies not so much in the plot as in qualities of the performance. In adopting this approach, I have drawn heavily on folklore and particularly on the performance tradition that has been influential since the late 1960s to early 1970s (see examples and reviews in, for instance, Bauman *Verbal*, Bauman *Story*, Ben-Amos and Goldstein, Fine, Fine and Speer, Finnegan, Lindfors, Paredes and Bauman, and a more recent review of performance issues in African oral literature in Okpewho). Fine (166–203) notes that the performance tradition sought to rectify a situation in which priority had been given to decontextualized, written accounts of folklore. Amongst other things, these presented an impoverished picture of traditional stories and other verbal art forms. More recently folklorists have seen storytelling as a highly contextualized practice, in which it is important to take into account how stories are performed, the interaction between storyteller and audience, how performances change in different contexts and so forth. My own analysis is consistent with this approach, although I prefer to see certain performance features not simply as contextual but as part of a highly complex composite story text.

In analyzing *A Man Amongst Men* I became interested in how Jan combines different elements: the choice of language code, features of verbal language, vocal features, and visual features, to create such a composite text. The combination of different modes is a pervasive feature of Jan's performance. It affects all aspects of the story, from the use of well-known stylistic techniques, such as repetition or parallelism to Jan's "management" of her interaction with the audience. In this chapter the focus is on how Jan takes on and represents different personae in the story.

Representation of Personae in the Verbal, Visual, and Vocal Elements of the Story Text

As is frequently the case in oral narrative performances, Jan does not simply recount the events in her stories. To a large extent, she also enacts these stories, taking on the voices of different characters. The narrator role can also be seen as a composite that is itself made up of different voices. Hill ("The Voices"), for example, distinguishes between different narrator voices or "self-laminations." Subsequently, I am focusing on

Jan's representation of different personae,[3] i.e., different aspects or facets of the narrator and different characters. Furthermore, I am also examining how this is accomplished through a combination of verbal and nonverbal textual elements.

As narrator, Jan both recounts and orchestrates the events that make up the story. Although she has quite a large area in which she could move around, she occupies a relatively small amount of space. This forms a story space or, more accurately, a time space, i.e., where events take place within the story time. This is where Jan, as narrator, retells events. From here she can also refer out to other times and places; she brings different characters into the story space and sends them away again. As part of this role, Jan needs to maintain a relationship with the audience, i.e., by encouraging audience participation, from time to time bringing the audience into the story, for instance, as villagers clapping and ululating. This recounting and orchestrating role comprises Jan's *retelling* persona. Jan sometimes steps out of this role to comment on events as an aside to the audience. The term *commentator* accurately describes this persona.[4] As narrator, Jan also explains things to the audience and instructs its members that (i.e., in ululating) this is her *teaching* persona. Finally, Jan embodies nine different characters or sets of characters in the story.

It is possible to gain an initial impression of the extent to which Jan takes on different personae by looking at the verbal story text: Table 1 below shows the number and percentage of words uttered by different types of personae, and table 2 shows the number and percentage of speaking turns taken by different characters in the story.

Table 1. Words uttered by different personae in *A Man Amongst Men*

Total words in narrative	2999	100%
Words in narrator's retelling persona	1865	62.2%
Words as commentator	63	2.1%
Words as teacher	79	2.6%
Words in characters' personae[5] (i.e., direct speech - 71 speaking turns)	932	31.0%
(Ideophones[6]/iconic representations of sounds)	60	2.0%

Table 2. Speaking turns taken by different characters

Hunter	21	29.6%
Hunter's wife	19	26.8%
Wife of 1st giant	11	15.5%
1st giant	7	9.9%
2nd giant	4	5.6%
1st giant's baby	2	2.8%
Men in field	2	2.8%
Men building	2	2.8%
Villagers	3	4.2%
Total turns	71	100%

NOTE: The three villagers' turns are ululations—they do not include conventional "speaking turns"; They clap and sing in a Nigerian language.

Even such a simple exercise as this raises questions as to what counts as the verbal text of the story because the boundaries between verbal and other components blur in several respects. What counts as a word, for instance, is not straightforward. There were several "near words" in characters' speaking turns that have been counted as words in table 1 (see note 5). In Jan's retelling persona the position of what are sometimes termed *ideophones* is unclear because sometimes these are close to conventional words (i.e., *boom*) and sometimes less so (i.e., *krrrpah*). However, if word-like forms such as *krrrpah* are included, what of sniffs, burps, and eating noises? Then, if sniffs, burps, and eating noises are included, why not clapping? There seems to be a functional distinction here: Sniffs, burps, and eating noises, although they are not strictly verbal, do have similar functions to words in the text (see Swann "'Text' and 'Context'"). Clapping is used to establish a rhythm and therefore has been grouped under "music" as a distinct textual element. All of these noises form part of the embodiment of different characters in the story. Whereas I have made a distinction between different personae, in the case of sniffs, burps, and eating noises, the boundaries between personae blur because these can be seen as the narrator as reteller describing the actions of characters but also possibly as characters uttering in their own voice.

Focusing on the verbal elements of the story text inevitably downplays several performance aspects, such as singing, ululating, and the audience involvement associated with them. While these aspects are hard to represent, they are in fact highly important and probably among the more memorable parts of the event. Conversely, some elements that would normally be analyzed as verbal seem less important, i.e., the actual words of songs sung in a Nigerian language by certain characters in the story.

Despite the boundary blurring mentioned above, it was necessary in analyzing the story to distinguish between the subsequent five different textual elements, assuming that the story can be considered as a composite text:[7]

1. selection of a language variety or code: in this case whether the storyteller speaks in British English, an African-accented English or an African language (in her Anansi stories Jan alternates between British English and Creole);
2. the verbal component: the selection of words and grammatical structures that make up the spoken text;
3. the vocal component: paralinguistic features such as tone of voice, pitch level and range, loudness, and speed;
4. the visual component: features such as facial expression, gaze, gesture, other bodily movement, body orientation (i.e., which way Jan is facing) and "stance," which is the overall body shape adopted by Jan;
5. the musical component refers to the rhythmic quality evident at certain points in the performance, i.e., in Jan's opening greeting to the audience; it also includes singing (Jan, unlike some storytellers, does not have any musical accompaniment); formally, this could probably be described using the features listed above under vocal component, but within music these sound different—music seems qualitatively different from vocal elements in speech; music, as identified here, also has a visual element, i.e., clapping, which is partly visual, and body movement; in combination, these help establish rhythm.

These components are still not adequate to describe the overall performance: It has to be decided how widely to define the story text, for instance, whether to include clothing, seating arrangements, layout of the performance area, and so forth. Nevertheless, the present analysis is still relatively narrow, focusing on the verbal part of the text and elements that closely intersect with it. Jan manipulates these components but also the verbal language to convey the actions and events that make up the story.

Jan's switches between the narrator's personae and the personae of different characters are accomplished in the verbal and other elements of the text, and they, in turn, require coordination between the different textual elements. A character's speaking turn is almost always represented as direct speech, explicitly introduced by the narrator: "he would say"... or "she said. . . ." Switches between the narrator and other personae are marked by a shift in accent in that the narrator speaks in British English, whereas the characters speak in an African-accented English. In other respects, the characters have distinctive voices and distinctive embodiments. Specifically, their tone of voice, facial expression, stance, and gestures differentiate among them and indicate, for each character, their physical characteristics, personality, emotions, actions, how these are carried out, and their general perspective or outlook on people and events. There is some similarity between different characters, i.e., between the hunter's wife and the wife of the first giant; the two giants; some men hoeing in a field and men building. These similarities play an important part in the story in that they are a form of repetition or parallelism, a device frequently used in oral narrative and other verbal art forms.

Jan's adoption of different personae is illustrated in the extract below, where she switches the narrator from the hunter and to the hunter's wife.[8]

The following legend should be used in reading all the following tables:

1. The narrator's retelling voice is in plain text; the characters' voices are in italics
2. Italics = mimetic representation of character
3. *indicates a point in the transcript referred to in the visual/vocal column
4. A = audience; N = narrator; H = hunter; HW = hunter's wife
5. " " = narrator's commentator persona as in table 5.

Table 3. Switching between different personae in *A Man Amongst Men*

	Narrator	Characters	Visual/vocal info.
11	... now (.) this hunter was a very vain and boastful man and after he *heard the people singing his praises and after he *heard the women ululating he would *uproot young trees and hold them high above his head and he would say		orients towards A; *both hands raised in slightly circular movements (twice) *uprooting gesture; brandishes trees; still in N's voice.
12		ha ha ha hhh truly I am a man amongst men	switch to H's voice–his body, face; still facing A; embodiment outlasts spoken words;
13	he would throw the tree down and he would *walk into his house and he would beat his chest and he would say to his wife		looks down, throws tree; *hands move forward; beats chest
14		ha ha ha hhh I am a man amongst men	switch to H's voice, body
15	his wife would say		
16	[laughter]	every day it's the same thing you come home you uproot trees you frighten the children you kick the dog you come inside you make your noise *ha ha ha I am a man amongst men	switch to HW — higher pitch; posture slightly more stooped; addressing H but facing A; *'takes off' H

The extract comes from near the beginning of the story. Jan has described how the hunter returns to his village to be greeted and praised by the villagers. As the extract begins Jan talks directly to the audience. She is in the narrator's retelling persona throughout this first contribution, though her initial bodily stance is consistent with the hunter's attributes and the hand movements on "heard" might indicate the sounds heard by the hunter. From "uproot" she takes on the hunter's actions, though still in the narrator's voice. At "ha ha ha" (12), with the beginning of the hunter's speaking turn, she switches entirely into the hunter's persona: This is a strong embodiment, marked by a switch in accent and involving the hunter's tone of voice, facial expression, stance, and physical actions. Specifically, the hunter is portrayed as loud, proud, large, and powerful. She switches back to the narrator's persona in turn 13. She takes on the narrator's voice, though she still partly embodies the hunter, echoing the actions described in the spoken text. She throws down the tree; on "walk" she moves her hands forward indicating the direction of movement and possibly as though to open a door or part a curtain, and she beats her chest. In turn 14 she moves into a complete embodiment of the hunter. She switches briefly back to the narrator at turn 15, then into the hunter's wife's persona at turn 16. As with the hunter, this is a strong embodiment. Jan takes on the hunter's wife's stance, facial expression, and tone of voice. Of particular importance is her attitude toward her husband, conveyed by her tone of voice, stance, and facial expression as much as by the words she utters. Clearly, she is clearly exasperated by his arrogance.

Embedded Representation. Jan takes on the personae of the narrator (as reteller) and of two different characters. However, there is a further embedded system of narration/representation in that one character, the hunter's wife, also (re-) narrates "the story so far" and takes on another persona, that of the hunter. This switch introduces an alternative perspective or "take" on the hunter as we have seen him portrayed by the narrator and appearing as a character in his own voice. Now we see him through another character's eyes as his wife ironically recapitulates his actions and rearticulates his words. This rather disparaging and mocking portrayal makes an immediate impact on the listeners who are seen in their laughter, and it probably affects how the hunter is perceived thereafter.

"Taking on" and "taking off." The hunter's wife, in taking on another persona, does not do so in the same way as Jan in her earlier representation of the hunter. Whereas evaluation can never be absent from the representation of personae in a narrative, the evaluative element is much stronger in the hunter's wife's representation: The difference here seems to correspond to a commonsense distinction between "taking on" a particular character and "taking someone off." It might be more accurate to say that, whereas the hunter's wife is quoting her husband, she is still speaking "in her own voice."

Jan, as narrator, also occasionally "takes off" other people. This may include the audience, as in the extract below. Here, Jan has talked about the tradition of Anansi stories, which are also part of her repertoire. She then switches to begin her performance of *A Man Amongst Men*:

Table 4. "Taking on" and "taking off" distinction, example 1

1	well after all of that I'm not going to tell you an Anansi story to begin with [laughter] that was just to whet your appetite I want you to wait ok I want you to be going *'*oh go on go on*' the first story I'm going to tell you comes from Nigeria ...	N addresses A directly; gazes round A; * hands together, pleading; voice also pleading;

At a later point in the story, when the hunter is fleeing from the first giant and encounters a second giant in a clearing, Jan switches from taking on the persona of the giant to taking him off as narrator in an aside to the audience (see table 5).

The "taking on"/"taking off" distinction is less evident in the verbal component of the text: In a conventionally written text, both forms of representation would be shown as direct speech, though the distinction might be inferred by the reader. It is rendered unambiguous in the story text because of clear differences in the vocal and visual elements.

Table 5 "Taking on" and "taking off" distinction, example 2

192	the giant said	
193		*ah I am the only man amongst men around here you come you sit here right here next to me*
194	"now if a giant says to you you *come here you sit here right next to me what do you do [laughter] you go and you sit there right there next to him"	* mimics G's voice ironically; gaze directly to A

Interpenetration of Narrator and Character Personae

I mentioned earlier that, in the verbal component of the story text, there is a lot of direct speech. Characters' contributions are almost always introduced by "he said" or "she said." There is no ambiguity about who is speaking. The narrator/character distinction is also maintained in the choice of language code: either a British or an "African" variety; in the vocal component, by tone of voice; and in aspects of the visual component, i.e., stance and facial expression. The visual component also, however, allows for greater complexity and some ambiguity. Jan needs to strike a balance, through the narrative as a whole, between representing characters and their activities and orienting toward the audience, checking on their response and involving them in the story.[9] This is particularly evident in the visual component.

Jan relates directly to the audience in her teaching and commenting personae. She addresses the audience unambiguously, maintaining her gaze and her body orientation toward its members. The extract with the giant provides a brief illustration of this. As reteller, Jan's gaze and body orientation tend to be toward the audience, though she may shift her gaze when representing a particular action. The example below (table 6), shows her shifting between direct address to the audience and representing the actions of a character, the hunter's wife:

Table 6. Interpenetration of narrator and character personae, example 1

	Narrator	Characters	Visual/vocal info.
38	*one day as *normal the *wife the *woman she took her calabash and went to the well to try to draw water for the day's cooking and cleaning and washing when she got to the well she *put her calabash down she took hold of the rope that was attached to the calabash at the bottom of the well and she pulled* *but for some reason on this day she could not pull the calabash up she pulled and she tugged and she heaved she put her foot against the side of the well and she pulled and she tugged* but she *could not pull up the calabash she could not draw water		gaze directly on A; *index raised, in turn, to center, her left, right and center; pulls then stops, *turns directly to A to address them; doing action, looks where she's pulling but also orients towards A; *dusts off hands; addressing A more directly;

When Jan makes a complete switch into the persona of a character, her orientation towards the audience weakens: Now characters are addressing and relating to other characters, not the audience. However, she still needs to monitor and secure the involvement of her audience. A frequent pattern in the representation of characters in the story is for characters to interact with one another while Jan maintains "half an eye" on the audience. For instance, a character might begin speaking by addressing another character, then look up to allow Jan to take in the audience, as in turn 161 (table 7), and turn 20 (table 8); or address another character while also, simultaneously, orienting towards the audience, as in turn 18 (table 8).

Table 7. Interpenetration of narrator and character personae, example 2

	Narrator	Characters	Visual/vocal info.
160	*And the giant sat up and looked down and saw this little man sitting on his stomach he said*		
161		*ah who are you and what are you doing here*	starts by addressing person on tummy then looks up

Table 8. Interpenetration of narrator and character personae, example 3

	Narrator	Characters	Visual/vocal info.
17	She said		
18		*one day this thing will be your downfall you mark me one day this thing will be your downfall you remember the saying when trouble sleeps young man he go wake (him) what (there) he go find wahala wahala big big trouble what you know you are a woman go in the kitchen and cook my dinner*	addressing H with index, but pans round A, index to different points (i.e., addressee isn't in one spot);
19	(he said)		
20		*What you know you are a woman go in the kitchen and cook my dinner*	Looks down and to the side to W; then up, disdainful expression (this also means H orients slightly more to A)

The personae in the story are, therefore, not as fixed as might appear from the verbal element of the text. There is some "leakage" between personae. This is the case, for example, when characters are speaking, and the narrator/reteller is, to some extent, hovering behind them and occasionally peeping out of his or her eyes. Conversely, when retelling the story, Jan as narrator partially embodies the actions of the characters she is describing, as is shown in the narrator columns of the transcripts given. This leakage stems, I think, from the multifunctionality of the story performance. Jan needs to recount the events of the story and also to take on the personae of different characters to ensure that she is maintaining the interest of the audience and sometimes to interact with them directly. These functions are more or less salient at different points in the story. For example, Jan interacts more directly with the audience in her narrator roles. However, but they are never entirely abandoned—even when taking on different characters, it is important to keep "half an eye" on the audience.

The evidence from *A Man Amongst Men* demonstrates the value of including systematic information about nonverbal elements in the analysis of performed oral narratives. This is not to suggest that all storytellers use visual and vocal elements in a similar way as Jan Blake. Undoubtedly, storytellers, clearly, have very different styles. Even if they are relatively still, for instance, storytelling is partly a visual art, and this stillness will be an important part of the performance. In Jan Blake's case, visual and vocal elements, along with other elements such as music, which are not included in the current analysis, are highly salient and are also closely integrated with the verbal part of the text. When one focuses on the functions of different textual elements, it becomes apparent that the relationship between verbal and nonverbal elements is quite intimate. Specifically, in a multifunctional text, similar and/or complementary functions are fulfilled by different components. This concept applies to just about any aspect of storytelling, but it has been illustrated here with respect to the way Jan represents different personae in the story.

There has been considerable interest in the relationship between personae or "voices" in written literary texts, and particularly in the ways in which these may be drawn on to represent different perspectives or points of view. Blurring the boundaries between narrator and character voices, for instance, may allow an author to conflate or to play on the ambivalence between different evaluative perspectives (see Vološinov's discussion of the role of "quasi-direct speech"). Coming from a rather different tradition, Leech and Short, in their classic account of *Style in*

Fiction, suggest that an author's representation of the speech or thought of others (i.e., characters in a novel) runs along a cline, from the narrator's representation of a speech act to "direct speech," in which a character is directly quoted, and then to "free direct speech," in which a character is quoted without an indication of the narrator's reporting voice, i.e., without being introduced by an expression such as "she said ... " (318–36). Leech and Short's contention is that the further away we get from the narrator's representation of a speech act, the less the reported speech appears to be under the control of, or mediated by, the author. In the middle of Leech and Short's cline comes "free indirect speech," an ambiguous form in which it is difficult to determine whether the words used belong to the narrator or to another person who is being cited. (Leech and Short's model has been refined in later publications, e.g., Short et al.)

Set against this relative complexity, the verbal representation of speech in *A Man Amongst Men* seems straightforward because it is always clear, in the verbal text, who is actually speaking. However, there is leakage and therefore ambiguity between narrator and character personae at the nonverbal level. Furthermore, nonverbal elements convey an evaluative perspective that is not evident in the verbal text. This is one example of the way that nonverbal elements in this sort of performed narrative take on some of the functions that would be fulfilled entirely by verbal language in conventional written literary texts. At one level, this supports folklorists' contention that performance features need to be taken into account by analysts to avoid giving an impoverished interpretation of oral narratives. However, it also throws into question what we count as text and as performance. All vocal and some, but not all, visual elements of a performance are so closely integrated with the verbal element that, in combination, they may be regarded as a composite "story text." Once one begins on such a multimodal analysis, however, the boundaries around texts begin to crack because it is not at all clear where "text" stops and something else—performance or context—begins.

Notes

1. This essay draws on a longer and more detailed analysis of the same story: see Swann "'Text' and 'context' in an oral narrative, " 2001.
2. Abrahams points out that things are also different in contemporary urban settings in Africa; specifically, stories are still told but turned into performances, often by professional or semi-professional storytellers for an evening's entertainment. This may give rise to generic change. Because storytellers do not know their audience, local references can't be made, nor can known people be alluded to or parodied—there is recourse to more stock characters. Stories may also be spun out, with more elaborate detail and more sophisticated musical accompaniment.
3. I am using the term *personae* in preference to alternatives such as *voices* to emphasize that these are enacted or embodied, because the visual component is highly important. I also want, at some points in the analysis, to distinguish different components of the story text, e.g., to distinguish visual and vocal elements.
4. Such comments are evaluative and constitute part of the evaluation in the narrative framework set out by Labov. There is, however, an evaluative element running through the story as a whole. I have used the term *commentator* to emphasize that this involves making explicit comments to the audience.
5. Words in characters' personae include 41 "near words" such as "ah" or "ha" as well as ululations (there are three of these); they do not, for the moment, include the words of songs sung in a Nigerian language.
6. Ideophones are the iconic representations of sounds made by characters (but not characters' vocalizations). Some of these are recognizable as words with agreed spellings (e.g., "boom boom boom" as the giant's footsteps shake the earth); others are borderline (e.g., "krrrpah krrrpah krrrpah" as the giant fells trees); and some would not normally be classified as words (e.g., a sniff or a burping sound).
7. There are several other ways of carving up this terrain: for a discussion, see Finnegan.
8. Some analysts of folklore narratives (e.g., Elizabeth Fine) have been concerned to find an ideal method of representing performance features. Fine terms this *intersemiotic translation*—an attempt to represent all the qualities of a performance in a written transcription to the extent that a reader would be able to reconstruct the actual performance. I have adopted a much more selective approach here, recording the verbal text in conventional spelling along with those nonverbal features that seem particularly relevant to the analysis.
9. The distinction I am making here corresponds more or less to Halliday's "ideational" and "interpersonal" functions of language (see Halliday xiii).

Works Cited

Abrahams, Roger. *African Folktales*. New York: Pantheon Books, 1983.
Bauman, Richard. *Story, Performance and Event*. Cambridge: Cambridge University Press, 1984.
———. *Verbal Art as Performance*. Rowley, MA: Newbury House, 1977.
Ben-Amos, Dana, and Kenneth S. Goldstein, eds. *Folklore: Communication and Performance*. The Hague: Mouton, 1975.
Fine, Elizabeth C. *The Folklore Text: From Performance to Print*. Bloomington and Indianapolis: Indiana University Press, 1984.
Fine, Elizabeth C., and Jean Haskell Speer, eds. *Performance, Culture, and Identity*. Westport, CT: Praeger, 1992.
Finnegan, Ruth. *Oral Traditions and the Verbal Arts: A Guide to Research Practices*. London: Routledge, 1992.
Halliday, M. A. K. *An Introduction to Functional Grammar*. 2nd ed. London: Arnold, 1994.
Hill, Jane H. "The Voices of Don Gabriel: Responsibility and Self in a Modern Mexicano Narrative." *The Dialogic Emergence of Culture*. Ed. D. Tedlock and B. Mannheim. Urbana and Chicago: University of Illinois Press, 1995.
Labov, William. *Language in the Inner City: Studies in the Black English Vernacular*. Philadelphia: University of Pennsylvania Press, 1972.
Leech, Geoffrey N., and Michael H. Short. *Style in Fiction: A Linguistic Introduction to English Fictional Prose*. London: Longman, 1981.
Lindfors, Bernth, ed. *Forms of Folklore in Africa: Narrative, Poetic, Gnomic, Dramatic*. Austin: University of Texas Press, 1977.
Okpewho, Isidore. *African Oral Literature: Backgrounds, Character, and Continuity*. Bloomington and Indianapolis: Indiana University Press, 1992.
Paredes, Americo, and Richard Bauman, eds. *Toward New Perspectives in Folklore*. Austin: University of Texas Press, 1972.
Short, Mick, Elena Semino, and Jonathan Culpepper. "Using a Corpus for Stylistics Research: Speech and Thought Presentation." *Using Corpora for Language Research: Studies in the Honour of Geoffrey Leech*. Ed. J. Thomas and M. Short. London: Longman, 1996.
Swann, Joan. "'Text' and 'context' in an oral narrative." *CLAC* Working Papers in Language and Communications. Centre for Language and Communications, Open University: UK, 2001.
Vološinov, V. N. *Marxism and the Philosophy of Language*. 1929. Trans. Ladislav Matejka and I. R. Titunik. Cambridge: Harvard University Press, 1973.

Contributors

Erika Behrisch is a doctoral candidate at Queen's University in Kingston, Ontario. Her dissertation, "Voices of Silence, Texts of Truth: Inuit Oral Testimony and the Lost Franklin Expedition," examines the representation and transformation of Inuit oral testimony in government documents, Victorian reportage, and popular literature on the lost Franklin expedition, 1845–1860. She has also written on Lady Franklin's involvement in the international search for her husband and nineteenth-century travel literature.

Irene Maria F. Blayer holds a Ph.D. in linguistics from the University of Toronto and is an associate professor in the Department of Modern Languages, Literatures, and Cultures at Brock University. Her main areas of research are Portuguese and Spanish dialectology as well as comparative studies in Romance linguistics within a historical context. Her current research interest also includes oral testimony, narrative, and identity.

Elena De Costa is an associate professor of Spanish and Chair of the Department of Modern Languages and Literatures at Carroll College in Waukesha, Wisconsin. She is the author of *Collaborative Latin American Popular Theatre: From Theory to Form, from Text to Stage* (1992) and a number of articles on Latin American literature. She is currently working on a manuscript, in which she studies visual and sound constructs in contemporary Hispanic poetry.

Corrado Federici holds a Ph.D. from the University of Toronto (1977) and is currently a full professor of Italian at Brock University in St. Catharines, Ontario, where he has been teaching since 1972. His research interests are primarily in the areas of modern Italian poetry, literary theory, and translation. He has published numerous articles and book chapters on writers such as Eugenio Montale, Giorgio Bassani, Luigi Pirandello, Giacomo Leopardi, Dacia Maraini, and Umberto Eco. He has recently published a translation of essays by Luciano Nanni, *The Power of Communication: Essays on Adespotic Aesthetics* (Lang, 2000).

Nila Friedberg is a doctoral candidate in the Department of Linguistics at the University of Toronto. Her major interests are in phonology, Slavic metrics, Russian verse theory, and Algonquian linguistics. She is an editor (with B. Elan Dresher and Michael Getty) of the forthcoming volume *Formal Approaches to Poetry: Recent Developments in Generative Metrics*. Her publications include "Foreign Accent in Brodsky's Verse," forthcoming in C. Kueper (Ed.), *Meter, Rhythm and Performance* (Peter Lang, Frankfurt).

Debi Keir-Nicholson, a graduate of Ryerson University, is the recipient of numerous awards from the Ontario Arts Council to promote the art of storytelling. She is founding member of the Dundas Storyspinners, member of the Storytellers School of Toronto, member of the Arts Council of Ontario, and the Hamilton-Wentworth Regional Arts Council.

Janet Maybin is a senior lecturer at the Open University, Milton Keynes, England. She has published a number of articles from her own research into children's construction of knowledge and identity through informal talk and has also edited books and published articles about social aspects of literacy. She has written extensively for Open University course materials at the undergraduate and postgraduate level.

Monica Sanchez is an assistant professor in the Department of Applied Language Studies at Brock University. She has a doctorate in linguistics from the University of British Columbia. Her two disparate areas of research are syntactic theory and the verbal art of storytelling. In addition to her academic pursuits, she is an active storyteller, performing at guild meetings, conferences, and concerts across the country.

Karen Seago is a senior lecturer at the University of North London, where she teaches German and English literature and translation studies. She has published widely on folk and fairy tales, feminist and literary revisions of fairy tales, in the work of Angela Carter, and on the reception of the Grimms' fairy tales in England. Contributions to encyclopedias include the *Oxford Companion to Fairy Tales* and the forthcoming

Routledge Encyclopedia of Women's Studies. She has also published extensively on language learning and is coeditor of a book on intercultural competence, *Target Culture—Target Language?*

Kay Stone has recently retired as professor of folklore in the English Department at the University of Winnipeg. She has also been a professional storyteller since 1974, performing in Canada and the United States. She has written numerous articles on folktales as literature, women and folktales, and professional storytelling. Her book-length study of storytelling, *Burning Brightly: New Light on Old Tales Told Today*, was published in 1998.

Brian W. Sturm, an assistant professor in the School of Information and Library Science at the University of North Carolina at Chapel Hill, has been sharing stories with children and adults for over ten years. His interest in modeling storytelling and storylistening—and the light trance states they can induce—has grown from watching people sit unmoving and scarcely breathing while listening to stories. He has published other articles on this storylistening trance in such journals as *The Journal of American Folklore, Storytelling Magazine,* and *School Library Media Research,* and he has just finished a book chapter on the reading trance. He has also co-authored a motif index of children's folktale collections with Margaret Read MacDonald, entitled *The Storytellers Sourcebook, Volume 2*, published by Gale (2001).

Joan Swann is a senior lecturer in the Centre for Language and Communications in the Faculty of Education and Language Studies at the Open University, England. Publications include several books and papers on language and gender and more general aspects of sociolinguistics. Her most recent book is *Introducing Sociolinguistics* (2000, Edinburgh University Press, co-authored with Rajend Mesthrie, Andrea Deumert, and William L. Leap).

Ernesto Virgulti is assistant professor of Italian at Brock University, Ontario. He has publications in several areas, among them: *Literary Semiotics in Italy* (1986), *Narratology as a Pedagogical Strategy* (1990), a chapter on Seymor B. Chatman in *I discorsi della critica in America* (Roma: Bulzoni, 1993), a critical edition of Luigi Pirandello's *Cosí è (se vi pare)* (Éditions Soleil, 2001), and a book on idiomatic expressions in English and Italian.

Allyson Wenzowski works in the Department of Mechanical Engineering at McMaster University. She has been a member of Dundas Storyspinners for over seven years and is co-host of a weekly radio program devoted to storytelling. She has told stories in various settings, including museums, galleries, and schools and has conducted numerous workshops and seminars on storytelling techniques. A freelance writer, she is a member of the Storytellers School of Toronto, the McMaster Museum of Art, the Art Gallery of Hamilton, and the Hamilton-Wentworth Regional Arts Council.

Index

A

Aarne-Thompson, 4,
Abrahams, Roger, 145
Adams, Robert, 2
adultery, 86–87, 93–94
   contes d'adultères, 94
   fole amor, 87, 94
Alighieri, Dante, 95
Apocalypse, 31
Arctic
   Artic exploration, 59
   Arctic literature, 59
   Morley, Henry, 59, 70
   search for Franklin, 60
Aristotle, 31
Aschenputtel (Grimm), 105, 107–110, 113
Ashliman, D. L., 4, 12
Aubin, Georger, 120
autobiography, 42–48, 50, 55
   autobiographical genre, 47
   autobiographical writing, 43, 47
Autobiography of a Runaway Slave, The (Barnet), 51

B

Babyonyshev, Maria, 118
Bacchilega, Cristina, 72
Bakhtin, Mikhail, 89, 131, 137, 141
Barlach, Ernst, 102–103, 108–110
Barnet, Miguel, 44, 50
Barthes, Roland, 97
Battista, John R., 16, 26
Bauman, Richard, 54, 147
Beauty and the Beast (Madame de Beaumont), 83
Begg, Ian, 18
behavior, 16–17, 37, 62, 75–78, 80, 107, 135
   behavior codes, 44
   gender-specific, 72
   male, 78
   negative, 80
   perceptible behavior, 16
Ben-Amos, Dana, 147
Berman, Morris, 16
biography, 44, 50, 52
Bloomfield, Leonard, 118–119
Bly, Robert, and Woodman, Marion, 113
Boccaccio, Giovanni, 89, 91–92, 94–96
border, 3–5, 10
   border of genre, 1
   crossed, 2, 10–11
   crossing, 2, 10

geographic borders, 10–11
ideo-narrative, 6
imaginary, 3
of transformation, 1
oral/print, 2
personal border, 1
Boring, Edwin G., 16
Bórquez, Josefina, 46, 49
Bottigheimer, Ruth, 76
Boutière, Jean, 98
Brücke, The (artist group), 105
Burgos-Debray, Elizabeth, 47, 51
Burning Brightly (Stone), 2, 13

C

Campbell, Marie, 13
cannibalism, 87
　a means of last resource, 58
　cannibal analogy, 62
　cannibalistic act, 87
　cannibalistic behavior, 63
　Franklin expedition, 62–65, 67
　Rae's report of, 60
Carter, Angela, 82
Cat and the Mouse in Partnership, The (Grimm), 105
Chamberlin, J. Edward, 61
Chapone, Mrs., 79
Charybdis, 39
Châtelain de Couci (French poem), 97–98
Children of Sánchez, The (Lewis), 42
Cinderella (Perrault), 83, 105, 114
Cirlot, J. E., 108, 110–112

clause, 119–120, 123
　main clause, 119–120, 123
　subordinate clause, 119–120, 123
Clouston, W. A., 98
Coates, Jennifer, 137, 144
Collins, Chris, 118
Collins, Wilkie, 58–59, 63
conduct, 37, 63, 65, 68, 76–80
　codes of, 44, 76, 79
　manuals, 77
Connell, Robert, 135
consciousness, 6, 15–18, 20–25, 42, 47
　altered state of, 15–16, 18, 20, 22–24
　baseline, 16, 22–24
　discrete state of, 16
　disruptive forces, 17
　patterning forces, 17
　social, 42
　sociopolitical, 41, 43
　stabilizing forces, 17
　states, 16–17, 24
　storylistening trance, 18, 22, 25
　trance state, 21, 23–24
　transitional period, 17, 22
　waking state of, 15
conversational space, 130
courtly love, 86, 88
Crane, Lucy, 77, 79
criticism
　literary, 15, 27, 45
　reader response, 15, 46
　role of the reader, 36, 46
Csikszentmihalyi, Mihalyi, 15
Curious Girl, The (Stone), 105, 113

D

Dahlstrom, Amy, 118, 123
Das Herze (German poem), 89, 91, 94
Davis, Matilda, 77–79
Decameron, The (Boccaccio), 99
Dègh, Linda, 3
Derrida, Jacques, 29
   différance, 29
   différence, 29
devices, 46, 118–119, 125
Dickens, Charles, 58, 60–67
discourse
   free indirect discourse, 141
Disney, Walt, 2, 72, 81–82
Divine Comedy, The (Dante), 95
Dix, Otto, 102, 104, 111–112
double-voicing, 141
Dreamer Awakes, The (Kane), 102

E

Eaten Heart (legend), 86–91, 94, 97–98
Eco, Umberto
   deconstruction, 28–29
   esoteric knowledge, 32
   "hermetic drift," 28–29, 36, 38
   "hermetic semiosis," 34, 37
   intentio auctoris, 35
   intentio lectoris, 35
   intentio operis, 35
Ericsson, K. Anders, 18
evaluative function, 130–131, 142–143
experience
   lived, 17, 43
   remembered, 17
Expressionism, 102, 105, 110, 113
   German Expressionism, 105, 113

F

fabula, 31, 34, 40
fairies, 73–76, 78–79, 81
   community of, 76
   thirteenth fairy, 73–79
   Thirteenth fairy
      as persecutor, 75, 81
      as single woman, 79
      as wise woman, 76, 77, 82
      as witch, 80
      demonization of, 77, 81
      evil, 31, 37–38, 72, 77–79, 81–82, 105, 107, 109
      spiteful fairy, 73–75, 78
      surplus fairy, 73, 79
Fairy tales, 72–73, 82, 106–110, 113
   as genre, 82
   canon, 45, 82
   canonic tale, 73
   classic, 65, 72, 75, 158
   core motifs, 74
fanaticism, 28, 32
Favati, Guido, 98
femininity
   encoded into fairy tales, 82
   fallen woman, 79, 83
   representation of, 80–81
feminist, 72, 82
   criticism, 15, 46, 55, 63, 82
   revisionary rewriting, 82
   scholars, 3, 11, 30, 37
   writers, 29, 62, 79, 82

Fine, Elizabeth, 147
folklore, 1–2, 12, 15, 87, 146–147
  performance tradition, 147
folktale, 1, 4, 113
  African, 145
  Catalan, 2
  Marie Campbell's collection, 2
  Japanese, 2
  Russian, 9
Folktales and Society (Dègh), 3, 13
Foucault's Pendulum (Eco), 29, 32–35, 38
framing devices, 48
Francese, Joseph, 28
Franklin, Sir John, 58, 60, 70
  Arctic exploration, 59–60
  character, 33–34, 38, 47, 51, 59, 60–61, 63, 65, 67, 72
  dramatic representation, 64–66
  Erebus and *Terror*, 64
  expedition, 58–61, 63–66
  fate, 7, 43, 58–62, 66–67, 76
  journey, 4, 38, 54, 58, 64, 66, 111
  Lady Franklin, 68
  national hero, 59
  Richard Wardour, 64–65, 67
Freeling, Arthur, 79–80
Frozen Deep, The (Dickens), 58–59, 63–66
functionalism, 16

G

Galileo, Galileo, 38
Gardiner, Alfonso, 77
Geist, 102
Georges, Robert, 20
German Popular Stories and Fairy Tales (Taylor), 78
Gillies, Robert, 77–79
Gray, Louis H, 97
Grimm, Jacob and Wilhelm, 1, 2, 12–13, 73–75, 78, 81,105

H

heretical orders, 30
heretical reading, 30
hermeneutics, 39
Hill, Jane H., 147
Household Words (journal), 59–65
Huguenots, 1
Hunt, Margaret, 77–78, 81
Hymes, Dell, 119, 125

I

ideophones, 149
Indian Woman in Guatemala, An (Menchú), 43, 55
Infant Custody Bill, 80
Inferno (Dante), 95
Interpretation and Overinterpretation (Eco), 28
intertextuality, 29
Inuit
  Arctic Natives, 62
  Inuit character, 62
Island of the Day Before The (Eco), 29, 35–38

K

Kamenetsky, Christa, 76
Kaye, Jonathan, 118, 121

Kiss, The (Munch), 102–103, 106–107, 111
Kukla, Andre, 17, 26

L

Labov, William, 130
labyrinth, 30
Lady of the House of Love, The (Carter), 82
Lai d'Ignaure ou Lai du Prisonnier (Beaujeu), 87, 98
Lai Guiron (song of love), 87, 94
Lancelot and Guinevere (romance), 94
Lang, Andrew, 2, 5
Langfors, Arthur, 98
Languages
 Algonquian, 118
 Cree, 12, 120–121, 127–128
 Icelandic, 118, 128
 Ojibwe, 118, 120–121, 123, 125–127
 dialects, 120
  Eastern Ojibwa, 120
  Golden Lake Algonquin, 120, 128
  Ottawa, 70–71, 120
  Pikogan Algonquin, 120
Le Roman du Châtelain de Couci, 89, 91, 94, 97–98
Leech, Geoffrey and Short, Mick, 158
Leonie (Dix), 102, 104, 111–113
Lewis, Oscar, 42, 56
Limits of Interpretation, The (Eco), 28–29, 34–35, 40
literature

children's literature, 73, 78
committed literature, 50
Latin American, 41–42, 44, 50, 54–56, 162
pseudo-autobiographical Latin American narrative, 50
testimonial narratives, 41, 52
Lovelock, James E., 16
Lüthi, Max, 3

M

male gender roles
 king, 14, 76, 77, 91
 manliness, 84
Man Amongst Men, A (story), 145–148, 152, 154, 158–159
Marching Warriors (Nolde), 102, 104, 110
Marsh, Caryl A., 15
Matus, Gill, 79
Matzke, John, 97–98
Maybin, Janet, 130–131
Mazzotta, Giuseppe, 99
McLuhan, Marshall, 1
McMaster Museum of Art, 102, 104, 113–114
memory, 5, 17–18, 20, 42–44, 49
 historical, 41, 51
Menchú, Rigoberta, 43, 46–49, 51
Misreadings (Eco), 28
Moore, Katharine, 81
Morgner, Irmtraud, 82
Morley, Henry, 59
Mother Hulde (Grimm), 105, 109, 112, 115

Mother Trude (Grimm), 105, 108–109, 111–113
Munch, Edvard, 102–103, 106–107, 111
Myth, 33, 72, 74, 76
  Brünhilde, 74, 76
  Edda, 75
  fate, 74–76
  Greek, 74
  mythic-oral mediation, 75
  mytho-literary derivation, 74
  Nibelungenlied, 75
  Nordic, 74, 76
  Norns, 74–76
  Odin, 74, 76
  Siegfried, 75
  Thidrekssaga, 75
  Völsungasaga, 75
Mythologie (Grimm), 74, 84
mythology, 87, 97

N

Name of the Rose, The (Eco), 27, 29–31, 33, 35
narrative
  'absent voice,' 46
  Arctic, 60
  authorial voice, 44–45, 48
  collective, 42
  components, 94
  conjuncts in, 118, 120
  diegesis, 37
  documentary or nonfiction, 41
  English, Russian, and Icelandic, 126
  first-person autobiographical, 43
  framework, 41, 160
  minimal, 86
  motifs, 86, 88
  motivation, 82
  Native American, 120, 125
  narrator, 2, 9–10, 30, 32, 34–35, 37–38, 41–43, 48, 51, 53, 125, 137, 140–142, 147–149, 151, 153–159
    fictional, 9–10
    omniscient narrator, 47
  oral, 1, 119, 145, 147, 151, 158–160
  oral genres, 1
  oral history, 42, 45
  oral tradition, 1, 2, 98, 145
  pseudo-autobiographical Latin American, 50
  structure, 41, 89, 91
  style, 49
  substitutionary narration, 48, 55
  testimonial, 41–52, 61–62, 66, 68
    as social practice, 47
    audience of readers, 53
    autobiographical, 48
    testimonio, 42–47, 51
  text, 46
  units, 15
  voice, 43, 46, 53
Nolde, Emil, 102, 110
Norton, Caroline, 80
Novellino, Il (story), 88–89, 94

O

observations
  behavioral, 17
  phenomenological, 17
  repeated, 17

Of Grammatology (Derrida), 29
Olney, James, 47
Once Upon a Time (Lüthi), 3
Open Work, The (Eco), 28
Opera aperta (Eco), 28
Opie, Iona and Peter, 74
orality, 41, 44, 52
Our Lady's Child (Grimm), 105, 109

P

Palmegiano, E. M., 79
Paris, Gaston, 97–98
Paull, Mrs. H. B., 77, 78
Pekala, Ronald J., 17, 26
Perrault, Charles, 1, 13, 73, 75, 77, 81
Perspectives (Bacchilega), 72
Plain Letter, A (Norton), 80
Poetics (Aristotle), 31
Poniatowska, Elena, 49–50
Poovey, Mary, 80
Propp, Vladimir, 97
psychology, 15
Pyramus and Thisbe (Ovid), 95

Q

Queen Bee, The (Grimm), 105, 108–111
Queskekapow, Nathaniel, 12

R

Rae, Dr. John, 58, 60–61, 63, 65–69
  Nurse Esther, 64–67
  report to the Admiralty, 58, 60–61, 66
Ramamujan, A. K., 14, 26
Reinhold, Meyer, 97

report
  autobiographical, 42
  introspective, 17
  subjective, 17
reported dialog, 131
representation, 18, 29, 43, 64–
  didactic, 75
  embedded, 153–154
  of character, 151, 156
  of events, 138
  of speech, 159
  personae, 147–148
  "self-representation," 43
  union of the lover, 97
Rhodes, Richard, 118, 120, 123
Role of the Reader, The (Eco), 28
Rölleke, Heinz, 76
Romain, A., 75
Rosenblatt, Louise M., 15
Ruskin, John, 73

S

Saggi su Il nome della rosa (Cardini), 22
Sakesep, Jakemon, 89, 97–98
Samber, Robert, 73
Schoof, Wilhelm, 76
Schriften (Grimm), 74
Schutz, A. H., 98
Scylla, 39
Seitz, Gabriele, 76
semiotics, 27, 29
  transcendent signified, 32
  unlimited semiosis, 34, 36–37
  polysemy, 27
Semiotics and the Philosophy of Language (Eco), 27
Sigurdsson, Halldor A., 118

Six Walks in the Fictional Woods (Eco), 28
Sleeping Beauty (Perrault), 72–74, 80, 82
   Dornröschen, 73
   fairy tales, 72, 82, 106–107, 109
   innocent persecuted heroine, 72
   La Belle au bois dormant (French version), 73
Snow White (fairy-tale), 2–3
speech
   direct speech, 76, 148, 151, 154, 156, 158–159
   "free direct," 159
   "free indirect," 159
   "quasi-direct," 158
   reported, 131–132, 159
Starks, Donna, 118, 120
Stephen, Michele, 16
Stephens, Walter, 3
Stone, Kay, 1–2, 105, 113
stories
   Abrahams' collection, 145
   Anansi stories, 150, 154
   Boccaccio, 96
   children's, 131, 137, 142
   classic, 72
   conjuncts in, 119, 121, 123
   conversational, 130, 137
   cultural values, 131
   evolution of, 6
   experience of reality, 15
   exploring as tellers, 11
   figure of the witch, 82
   from oral to written, 2
   linked, 138
   medieval, 75
   moral judgments, 130
   motif, 105
   North Pole, 60
   Ojibwe, 125
   oral, 74
   performing, 14
   reception of, 91
   relationships between voices, 131
   state of consciousness, 21
   structural components, 94
   tales, 76
   themes, 113
   through a journey, 49
   traditional, 73, 147
   tragic love stories, 95
   variants, 82
story
   a told story into written form, 2
   dialogic relationship, 131, 135
   dialogic work, 143
   experience, 15
   recreate the, 11
   the realm of, 6
   told, 11
   waking state of consciousness, 15
   written, 2
storytelling, 2, 15, 18, 21, 47, 91, 102, 118–119, 125, 145, 147, 158
   act of, 47
   Andrews, Jan, 61
   collaborative, 46
   concert, 102
   event, 15, 21
   face-to-face, 6
   festivals, 18
   historical nature, 44

listening, 15
motifs, 91
Native American, 126
Ojibwe, 126
oral, 46
oral form, 2
power to entrance, 15
story listening, 21–22
storylistening experience, 18
storylistening trance, 18, 22, 25
storyteller, 13
style, 22
tellers and listeners, 6
testimonial, 42, 45
United States, 14
visual art, 158
Sugarhead, Cecilia, 119–120, 122–123
systems theory, 15–16

T

tales, 49, 59, 105–106
   courtly love tradition, 87-88
   Grimm's tales, 1–, 73, 76, 105, 108–109, 113
   Medieval tales, 86–87, 94
Tart, Charles T., 16, 17, 24
Tatar, Maria, 76
Taylor, Edgar, 73, 77, 78, 80
Tejera, Victorino, 28
Tepper, Sheri, 82
themes, 105–106, 137, 143
   of transformation, 113
Theory of Semiotics, A (Eco), 27
Tomashevsky, Boris, 97
Toolan, Michael, 141
Toward a Science of Experience (Kukla), 17
Toward an Understanding of (Georges), 20
Transition, The (Barlach), 102–103, 108–110
Tristan and Iseult (tragic love story), 87, 95
Trobadora Beatriz (Morgner), 82
Turnip, The (Grimm), 105, 108–109

U

Unspotted Snow (Morley), 59
Until We Meet Again (Poniatowska), 49, 51

V

Valentine, Randolph J., 118, 120, 123, 125
verbs, 119, 122–125
   conjunct verbs, 118–125
   independent verbs, 124
   nonverbal features, 160
   sound patterns, 119, 127
Vida of Guillem de Cabestaing, 89
voice
   anonymous, 42
   autobiographical, 46
   collective, 42, 45
   communal, 43
   individual voices, 131
   narrative, 53
   narrator, 147, 151, 157
   reproduced, 132–133
   testimonial, 43–44, 46, 48
   witness-participant-narrative, 53
Vološinov, V. N., 158

Von Strassburg, Gottfried, 98

W

Walkowitz, Judith, 79
Water of Life, The, 2, 4, 6, 10–11
Watson, John B., 16
Wehnert, Edward, 77–79, 81

White, Pamela, 18
Woodcutter's Child, The (Grimm), 105, 108–110, 111
word stream, 49

Z

Zipes, Jack, 83